The Misfit Miracle Girl

CANDID REFLECTIONS

Kate D. Mahoney

DIVINE PHOENIX

In coordination with
PEGASUS BOOKS

Divine Phoenix Books
PO Box 1001
Skaneateles, NY, 13152
www.divinephoenixbooks.com

First Edition: December 2016

Published in North America by Divine Phoenix and Pegasus Books. For information, please contact Divine Phoenix c/o Laura Ponticello, PO Box 1001, Skaneateles, NY, 13152.

This book is a work of non-fiction. Some names and identifying details have been changed to protect the privacy of individuals. Although the author and publisher have made every effort to ensure that the information in this book was correct at press time, the author and publisher do not assume and hereby disclaim any liability to any party for any loss, damage, or disruption caused by errors or omissions, whether such errors or omissions result from negligence, accident, or any other cause.

Library of Congress Cataloguing-In-Publication Data
Kate D. Mahoney
The Misfit Miracle Girl: Candid Reflections/Kate D. Mahoney– 1st ed

p. cm.
Library of Congress Control Number: 2016958262
ISBN – 978-1-941859-58-2
1. BIOGRAPHY & AUTOBIOGRAPHY / Women. 2. BIOGRAPHY & AUTOBIOGRAPHY / Personal Memoirs. 3. RELIGION / Comparative Religion/Religion and Spirituality. 4. MEDICAL / Healing. 5. HUMOR / Topic / Religion. 6. BODY, MIND & SPIRIT / Inspiration & Personal Growth. 7. FAMILY & RELATIONSHIPS / Life Stages / Adolescence.

10 9 8 7 6 5 4 3 2 1

Comments about *The Misfit Miracle Girl: Candid Reflections* and requests for additional copies, book club rates and author speaking appearances may be addressed to Kate D. Mahoney directly at www.katedmahoney.com.

Author photo credit – Johnson Camera
Got Miracle?® is a service mark registered to Kate D. Mahoney

Also available as an eBook from Internet retailers and from Divine Phoenix Books

Printed in the United States of America

Advance Praise

"In *The Misfit Miracle Girl: Candid Reflections*, Kate writes of the long journey toward understanding such a profound childhood moment. With each page, Kate projects the same qualities those who know her always find in her presence: Her words evoke a joyous and loving intensity, a searching wonder and humility, about her story and communion with the larger world."

~ Sean Kirst, Longtime Upstate NY columnist, journalist and author

"Kate's raw, beautiful truth is one of a life that has been made richer through the mess of pain and faith and struggle and miracles. It will touch you deeply."

~ Mary Ellen Clausen, Founding Director, Ophelia's Place

"Whenever she writes or speaks, she lays it all out on the table -- her love, her joy, her pain. She doesn't beat around the bush, and there's something to be said for that. Kate will always tell you the truth. And she tells it with a side of laughter, a glimmer of hope. She reminds us that we're human. She reminds us that we all make mistakes—and that's okay. She reminds us to find joy in difficult moments."

~ Alyssa LaFaro, Writer and editor, Chapel Hill, NC

"Kate doesn't wait for opportunities to present themselves, she creates her opportunity and then takes hold of that potential and makes it happen. She understands patience, and has a heart so full of love that more often than not she presses pause on her plans to take care of those around her. There has never been any doubt in my mind that the detours she has taken in life have only served to make her stronger, smarter and more determined to make an impact."

~ Allison Heishman, Associate Artistic Director, Azuka Theatre, Philadelphia, PA

Dedication

Mom, remember what Gretchen said.
I love you.
D

Note To The Reader

Stories have come to us in many ways throughout history: through music, cave wall drawings, sign language, interpretive dance, theater, painting or sculpture, poetry. We hand down our experiences with story, and each new audience will glean something different to pass on in their way to the future generations. Story is a gift to be given and shared. It is personal and often one-sided. My story, as the title suggests, is based on my memories before, during and after the label of "Miracle Girl" was placed on me.

I do not claim to be an authority on anything other than my own experiences. My recollections of events and experiences are my perceived truths. My words are my own, though they are perceptions, not necessarily facts.

Kate D. Mahoney is a miracle and she wants you to know you are too, even if that's not what you'd call it.

The Misfit Miracle Girl, Candid Reflections is an inspirational, humorous and inviting collection of essays that tell the story of Kate before, during and after surviving a terminal illness that came with it a decree from the Vatican and discharge papers stating her recovery cannot be explained medically.

Join Kate on a journey of discovery, transformation, calamity and noteworthy perspective. Her message to you, "What you think, what you feel and who you are always matters. You always have a voice."

Kate D. Mahoney is the author of *The Misfit Miracle Girl, Candid Reflections* and an International Speaker and Actorvist. Her recovery from Multi System organ failure was the first of two miracles elevating Mother Marianne Cope to Sainthood. Learn more and connect at www.katedmahoney.com.

In Order of Appearance

Introduction

Hi there!

"Chosen" never felt accessible to me, when I allowed others to determine what the weight of it should mean.

I think back to my life as a child. My bedtime prayer was, "God bless everyone and everything, living or dead, in this world or the next." I was taught many prayers and much about faith in my formative years; but this was a prayer I'd created for myself. It's been the core of my beliefs every day since.

In prayer—like all belief systems—we have an opportunity to transform. We ebb and flow. We are reaffirmed. We learn, we change, we grow.

I remain the woman my parents raised who believes all people deserve a life that affords them opportunities to provide for themselves and those they love, those who love them and those we don't love as much as we should. This choice is not always easy.

In my accessible memory, I was chosen before I asked to be. I was chosen before I agreed to be. I was chosen when I didn't want to be. For those of you who believe I did ask, agree and want whether I recollect it or not? Fair play to you; my story is as much about humanity as it is divinity.

It's a lot to ask one person to carry the burdens, fears, judgments, loves and hopes of a whole society on their back. I have been that person. I will continue to be that person. To me, that's what chosen is. I am chosen the same as anyone else, but it's taken time for me to own it.

Within that ambitious intention are days—simple, repeating days. There are no servants to dress me in robes; I pick up my own laundry off the floor, too. Every now and again, I open my eyes and immediately plan and plot for the minute I can crawl back into bed. More often than not my dog ignites a fire under me to get out the door to start our day.

We begin with my stretching, her assessment of my morning breath, our search for her leash or my sock. These things are not a grand miracle, but they are at times an attempt against seemingly insurmountable odds. Once outside, she sniffs and I take in the stillness of the morning, and the sunrise. We both enjoy the birds.

I know I am chosen, not for what I can do with the rest of my day, but for the reality that in that moment, I am actually given a gift in the presence and the power of an entire world going from night into day, all of which happens with or without my permission or acceptance.

The mundane nature of most days—working out, breakfast, dishes, emails, writing, grocery shopping, errand running, phone calls, meetings—these too are things I could compartmentalize and speak to as gifts, blessings and opportunities from which to learn and grow. In the grand scheme of things, they are. But when I'm stuck in traffic, the tub won't drain or I don't know where my next paycheck is coming from, my go-to is not typically a move associated with gratitude.

This is why I meditate. I didn't used to, but I actually need to mandate that silence in myself; otherwise, I'm prone to distraction or the temptation of calling someone an expletive out loud and to their face. My brand of chosen is more like an old shoe; it's worn but still walking and shows signs of occasionally kicking ass.

Whenever we can, my pup and I team up again for a sunset stroll, taking in the sounds and sights of the day, observing people winding down and settling in.

Invariably, there are things on TV I want to watch: news of the day both in reality and in theory. The impactful to the less impressive stories in the global community each have merits. Every voice is one of a person who believes they have something that needs to be heard.

When I turn out the light and put my head on the pillow, depending on my energy, I say prayers. Some are traditional and in my brain from childhood; others more a wish for people who spoke to me that day.

Regardless, I always say thank you. As the world goes once again from day to night, I may be chosen, but I'd be an ingrate not to acknowledge that which remains greater than me.

In this light, I welcome you to my story. It took me a while to get here, to this place where I live in a mindset that I am as human and imperfect as I am chosen and worthy. It's a total package deal with no expiration date and plenty of opportunity for continued growth.

The world we live in can feel at times to be fractured; but if we look at human behavior, we learn that we all have basic needs, understandable wants, hopes and dreams worthy of respect. Victim or survivor, thief or hero, parent or child—we all deserve to be heard, honored and loved.

I believe people can come together in the circumstances of humanity to embrace and move forward as one! Despite what on the outside would appear to be polarizing differences that might exist at times in our life, or within our communities, we can put aside judgments, and realize that we have more in common than our differences.

As you pick up and put down this book, trust that you'll always be reading what you're meant to. Because, you see, I think we are all chosen; we all end up where we are supposed to be.

And some might say that's a miracle…

Kate

I Call Her Mother

While I didn't own my relationship with her at the onset, I've come to believe Barbara Koob—aka Marianne Cope—and I were connected long before the Vatican declared my recovery a miracle attributed to her, binding us together in a very fancy, public way.

She has become my mentor, though we've never shared a tangible moment together in this lifetime. She continues to answer my questions, quell my fears, nudge me to where I'm meant to be, many times without my full knowledge or immediate understanding.

In my most wounded and broken state, I felt no connection to God. Yet I always found her to be within reach. She offered herself to me as a bridge, and I took her up on it, even when I didn't know where I was headed.

Because I am human, it took me a little time to put the pieces together. Because I am human and riddled with doubt and fear, sometimes she's believed enough for both of us.

You will join me in my story, growing up, against and in spite of my Catholic faith as I cultivated a bond that is as human as it is divine.

I don't expect you to fully embrace this relationship. In fact, I hope you challenge it as you read, because it means you're thinking about it. Thinking is good.

In a world made up of religions and beliefs historically rooted in love, it is the practitioners within them who have created the concepts of judgment and hate.

What you think or feel about my relationships isn't going to change any part of what I believe. However, dialogue around any of it helps us continue to find points of connection and unity.

Calling her "Saint Marianne" would be like calling my mother "Mrs. Mahoney." Most days, in my eyes, these women and my connection to them are the same, anyway. They both gave me life, love, security and shelter. One may give me money for the meter, but I assure you the other one helps me find the parking spot.

Mothers don't always have children in the traditional sense. Ask any person who has been mothered outside of society's norm if that bond is any less sacred. More often than not, you'll find a mother's love in any form has no borders or boundaries.

If we acknowledged the word Saint as universally as we do Mother, we'd be in quite a conundrum, having to calculate whose mother was doing better than the next, to define for us how we measure up. I'd need an abacus!

Everything from signs telling us coffee is hot to the title of Saint exists for a reason; the latter is a directive for respect and reverence, a testament to relationship and a job well done. Titles—like labels—create as much distance as they do definition.

Does a title really tell us everything we need to know? I don't believe so. It is almost impossible to reduce a person or their life's work to one word, whereas a lifetime of action, such as the act of mothering, can make quite an impact. Marianne Cope in life, and in death, mothered to all.

That's why I call her Mother.

Act I
Meet the Miracles

"There wasn't a fork in the road; there was an entire set of cutlery most times. Yet, I have never known a greater peace than being in the presence of my Mom and Pop."

Mother Of A Miracle

Mary Rose, my mom, is the eldest daughter of 14, seven boys and seven girls. The third child, she began her mothering duties in Ithaca, NY, at age 5, when my grandmother brought home the triplets.

Gramma said to Mom and her two sisters, "Here's a baby for you, a baby for you and a baby for you!" The directive to my mother was always that she would be the helper and responsible for the other siblings. As Mom said, "I did love it."

My grandparents were both raised Catholic, if you didn't sense that at the onset with the 14 children. Acquaintances in their youth, the two started dating casually in groups of friends as they got older. The engagement, like my grandfather, was simplistic, sweet and somewhat spur of the moment.

They sat at a table watching friends move to the music at a local soiree.

Grampa said to Gramma, "Maybe that will be us one day?"

"Dancing?" she asked.

"No…Married."

My grandfather, Tom, was the youngest boy of immigrant parents. His father, known to us as Dada, was from Italy. Dada started carrying water and ultimately became a giant in the railroad industry, creating a railroad ballast cleaning company; Grampa's mother, Nana, was from Ireland.

Family lore says Nana left a note for her family in the thatched cottage, indicating she was coming to America to become a nun. I'm not convinced that was ever the real plan.

My grandfather, the youngest of eight, was required to prove his worth in his own ventures before joining the family company officially. He started a frozen vegetable company. His vehicles were a combination mail truck and rickshaw, but evolved into trucks and brought in stable revenue.

Though he travelled back and forth from Ithaca to Syracuse already for the company, his proven business savvy as an individual earned him an equal spot at the table—with his father and brothers, and required the family to move to Syracuse.

My grandmother, Rose, was one of two siblings: she and her brother William, who we affectionately called Ham. From the time she was tall enough to reach the counter, she was her father's assistant at Knight's Meat Market. She was in charge of handing wrapped orders to the customers.

Poppy, my great-grandfather, was widely respected in his field for the humane treatment of animals, his support of community groups and sports teams. He was the butcher of choice for many, even those from New York City, for his kosher practices.

My great-grandmother suffered from scarlet fever in her youth. She was a force, a model of strength and value for my grandmother, despite her weakened heart. She died before Gramma and Grampa got married.

I don't believe the ache attached to the absence of her mother ever truly went away for Gramma.

My grandmother's Catholicism was as solid as my grandfather's, but perhaps weathered storms a bit differently because of her exposure to other religions by way of the market. Her best friend was Methodist, and the Church dictated she could not be an attendant in the wedding ceremony.

Yes, it was an era when people not only listened, but obeyed, the authority. I think that model affected her. I'm sure it's why we could have such frank discussions about religion and faith as I grew up, even if they were in private. These conversations about life and the world almost always took place in the kitchen as she taught me about different cuts of meat and how to prepare them.

Gramma set the example for how to manage a world in terms of self: as a woman, a mother, a wife and a community member.

Mom was 11 when the family settled in the Strathmore neighborhood of Syracuse, NY, after the move from Ithaca. She was enrolled at the Convent School, an institution run by the Third Order of Franciscans. My grandmother sat on about seven different parent-teacher associations, yet somehow managed to found the coffee shop and head up the auxiliary of one of the local hospitals, once led by a Franciscan nun called Mother Marianne Cope.

Gramma had a high aesthetic with great attention to detail. She said her novena daily, bestowing on all her loved ones a hope and blessing for security and safe passage through life.

Grampa exhibited devotion by way of light-hearted poetry, weekly mass followed by a myriad of breakfast sweets and evenings earnestly absorbing Catholic programming. After his death, we found an album containing copies of checks made out to parishes all along the eastern seaboard and across much of North America.

He was not a man of many words, but his laughter was contagious, his reach was infrequent but impactful and his faith was unwavering.

Gramma and Grampa had differing views and specific roles as it related to their children and grandchildren. The DNA makes most of us artists, in fields of food to fashion, teachers in education and industry. The tribal dynamic simply means that there are few people on the street we can't relate to.

It's a lot of live theatre.

In faith, some of my aunts and uncles remain devout to the Church and my grandparents' God; others consider themselves recovering Catholics; a few have a belief that connects them to earth and universe.

Gramma maintained to her death at age 94 that she had 14 only children, each with unique needs, wants and contributions for the world. It's not a shock to know that my mother's personal and professional path was one of early childhood education, research, support, development and mentorship from the bassinette to the board room.

Mom was named after the Blessed Virgin, and Gramma. She was as good a little Catholic girl as they come, with a strong sense of self from day one. Licking a lollipop after bedtime the night before her first communion, she walked up the aisle the next day to face the priests, believing flames would eventually melt the soles of her patent leather shoes. Upon confirmation, she silently dismissed the pledge not to drink until age 21 because she wasn't sure how she'd feel about drinking by the time she was that old.

By 21, Mom had completed courses at several colleges across the country. One transfer was simply because my uncle graduated and she had to find a college closer to home that semester so she could have a ride.

At each campus, Mom had to take the course Marriage in the Family, because the credits didn't transfer.

Her family and that faith served her well with each syllabus; but as she grew in her career, she did ponder Church protocols in context to young children. For example, confession: "Why would you send a child into a dark box with a stranger and tell them if they don't go, they'll go to Hell?"

She's not wrong to pose the questions, if you ask me. It's her ability to balance belief and behavior that helped her excel in her field and create a sense of stability for me. She was always willing to ask questions and learn more.

Is it any wonder that the girl who always wanted to solve problems and questions ended up with a guy (my father) who wanted to answer that call, too?

Mahoney

John was born the youngest of four children to Marion and RT. They lived on the south side of Syracuse, known to locals as The Valley. John was six years younger than his brother, the namesake of his father. The respective gaps were 10 and 11 years from his two sisters. He was to all, especially my grandmother, considered "the baby."

Born in 1899, Gram was the eldest sister of nine children. She took on the role of matriarch at age 15 when her mother died. Before her death, my great-grandmother Nellie, from Ireland, walked my grandmother through what her coming of age would be like, down to the preparation and hygiene surrounding her first period.

In the retelling of the occurrence, my grandmother would share that she was keenly aware of the magnitude of the moment and the importance of the instruction, especially given that this speech would be hers to tell her younger sisters for generations to come.

Gram accompanied her father, JP, also formerly of Ireland, to events, both social and professional. He was a contractor and often attended ribbon cuttings and celebrations of places he had built. She saved all those dance cards—along with a million other things a person can fit into a jam jar, complete with a rubber band seal.

She was her father's pride and joy and I think he was hers.

Amidst the sadness and the pragmatism of life on the farm without her mother, Gram would also share that Esther, her middle name, was in honor of the woman on the farm next door. She liked the woman. The name she said, "…was dumb."

Gram was a lifelong learner, with a deep faith for which she had no apology, defense or explanation. Her devotion was evidenced by the worn pages of her prayer book and the grip with which she held her rosary beads.

Every Lent, she would give up sweets, and convey to us the importance of tangible sacrifice. This, I believe, came in part from her living in and surviving the Great Depression.

Conversely, she also taught me how to handicap horses. She loved the races. Both my grandmothers did.

All these facets of my grandmother poured out of her and into her children. They each sopped up what they were meant to, or as she would say, "What God intended."

By age 3, little Johnny accompanied Gramma to her bridge games, where he recited all the names of the Presidents for her friends. He learned early that it felt good to please his mother and as he grew, their relationship became one of true solidarity; she was his confidant and he was hers. She fostered his love of learning and his interest in the world, and modeled for him what it meant to be a part of community.

She had been kicked out of school for walking out to attend a suffragette march while in high school. By extension, she celebrated my father's desire to engage in politics at a young age, challenge authority (within reason) and travel the world to see what it was all about.

She was willing in faith and practice to lift Pop up in success and comfort him in seeming failure. I think she did that for all her family.

The Mahoney faith family was tight—very Irish. All the priests knew they could come to my grandparents for a game of pick up (basketball), a good meal, engaging entertainment, stories or music. Plus, my grandfather always had a bottle of something under the kitchen sink that kept many a visitor happy, if not hydrated.

Witnessing these captivating conversations and reality that a priest was more than his vestments or his place on the altar made an impression on my father.

At age 12, he was president of the Catholic Interracial Council, an altar boy and a scout.

He couldn't have articulated it then, but the Jesuit training— that quest for knowledge and expectation for scholarship and stewardship—was shaping him in a more formal way for the life he would ultimately lead.

Graduating from a Jesuit school in 1959, my father left for Washington, D.C., to attend Catholic University and obtain a doctoral degree.

John Fitzgerald Kennedy was also transitioning in our nation's capital with an historic attempt to be the first Catholic in the White House.

If you happen to be an Irish Catholic of a certain age, you know that most homes had pictures of the Pope, Jesus and JFK. My grandparents' was no different.

Opting for the school of life rather than completing the degree program in a time of tremendous change, Pop took lots of posts in and around the Kennedy, Johnson and Clinton White Houses and remained active on Capitol Hill during the time of oppositional power.

Did I forget to mention? These Mahoney's were Irish Catholic Democrats, a species all their own.

Pop and Gram wrote letters back and forth to each other weekly. She commented on legislation and balanced it with an inquiry as to whether or not he'd met a nice Irish girl to bring home. Grampa would talk on the phone only to ask when Pop would be moving back home.

My grandfather's approach to fathering was less hands on. Admittedly, I have very limited memories of him, but I'm told he wasn't bookish; he was a scrapper who worked with his hands.

He loved to travel, but he wasn't worldly. He and my grandmother were very social, but he didn't attend events for or with my father as a kid. He never let my father touch anything, nor did he teach him how things were put together. He loved his kid and politics, having held office locally himself, but didn't understand or connect with my father's more academic and intellectual interests.

Later in life, my grandparents joined Pop on political junkets. One funny memory was of Grampa ordering Scalopini from a menu in Italy on Good Friday. He thought he'd ordered scallops only to have veal arrive to the table. Rather than throw out food, he ate the veal…and went to confession for eating meat on such a holy day. That was the model in those days.

Pop carried my grandfather's rosary ring with him all the time. After Grampa's death, he carried the perceived absence of interest from those formative years; I was at least 12 before I realized he was happy I was a daughter and not a son for whom he could make up the difference. A year that stands out would be one in which I got a baseball glove, leather oil and ball that preempted a game of catch. Don't get me wrong, I loved it; I just happened to have wanted a stuffed horse with a mane I could braid instead of a man-to-man talk in which I felt extremely ill-equipped on multiple levels.

Thank goodness there was another woman in John's life to help him further express the parts of him that were still a child as he began to raise one himself.

Match.Wit.

Mom knew she wanted a partner in life.

Every Friday night, a cohort of co-teachers or friends and a sister or two would go out to the bars in search of husbands. And every Saturday morning—often nursing the aftermath of husbandry requirements and several batches of Manhattans—they vowed to never do it again...until the following Friday.

One wintery Friday evening, Mom walked into a bar (it—along with her interest in Manhattans—is no more). The clouds of smoke and waves of people parted like the Red Sea to reveal "The man I knew I would marry."

"There was energy... a... charisma... magnetism and I was drawn to him instantly," she told me.

At no point did she seem to be romanticizing this encounter. She's very matter-of-fact as she recalls seeing my father for the first time.

"I just knew."

Pop tells his version of this same night with far less effusiveness than is typically delivered via his standard storytelling public persona. He's not reserved, exactly, indicating only to those who know him that meeting my mother is, in fact, such a powerful event that for a linguist such as himself, he's at a loss, as there are no words to convey her presence in his life.

Yet, true to form, raised in the generation in which emotions were never viewed as strengths, he says, "I kept getting letters from this Mary Speno, and I didn't know who she was."

There is guilt in his voice, acknowledging the allowance of this lie to utter and leave his lips as the sin it is. But he covers with default laughter. Mom smiles, knowing the depths of his soul so accurately that attempting to challenge his feelings—bringing into light his vulnerability—serves no purpose.

She knows he loves her; that's all that matters.

That crazy, snowy night ended with my parents at another dive bar where the waitress had Christmas lights in her hair. Mom's car only went in second gear, and her sister was with her.

These were not roadblocks to my father; he tagged a friend as a wingman, and at each red light between their meeting point and the end of the night, these two guys got out to push the car through every intersection.

What strikes me most when my parents tell this story is that they never refer to each other's looks.

Maybe it's because there is obviousness to my mother's beauty. She is her own signature blend of the American and Italian starlets of her time; she is breathtakingly yet unassumingly gorgeous.

My father, with his thick wavy dark hair and glistening eyes, has crooner intensity and similar appeal.

It can't be that their respective appearances didn't play a part, but they talk of laughter, shared values and little else when recounting that night—or their relationship since that night.

I maintain theirs was a story set in motion long ago. I can't help but feel there was a higher power orchestrating this point of connection, to which they willingly said, "Yes."

Speaking of I Do's, my parents' engagement is another event that set the tone of embracing relationship over grandiosity, or even minimal planning.

They were in Henderson Harbor, out with their usual band of theologians: legislators, realtors, house wives, farmers, mechanics, musicians and other levels of people who make up the world. They sat around the table, and as night turned to day, my mother began her mantra.

"Are you going to marry me?"

It started quietly but was received by a few like cannon fire.

"Do you think you'll marry me?"

The herd began to thin out.

"If you don't marry me, I'm going to go to Europe."

Mom had about $4 in nickels on her, so it's anybody's game to see if that veiled threat ever came to fruition.

"When do you think we will get married?"

"Okay! I'll marry you!"

Again, my father would tell the story as though he was defeated, but let it be known that for as impulsive as his temper could sometimes be, he was not a man in his personal or professional life to make a move that wasn't at least examined, if not prayed on, in regards to risk or reward.

He knew he needed and wanted my mother in his life. Of course, my mother beautifully capitalized on that, trusting herself to know that he just needed help to bring his feelings to the surface.

Mom ran back to her parents' cottage to wake them and share the wonderful news. My father passed out on the glider, in effort to get an hour or so of sleep before catching a flight back to Washington later that morning.

My grandmother leaned over my dad, her son-in-law to be.

"John, we're so excited! Before you go, don't you think you ought to go in and ask Tom for Mary's hand?"

Pop responded with less diplomacy than a donkey and more like that of an ass: "She asked me. Have her go ask my father."

Luckily, my grandmother had worked with livestock as a child. She acted as the conduit between the man who would give my mom away and the one who would whisk her away.

Pop had asked one of my uncles once what it was my grandfather did for a living. My uncle said that Grampa had weekly meetings in the back room of an Italian restaurant downtown, and on occasion went out to the rail yard.

Pop absolutely thought there was a chance that my mother was part of a low-level crime family, and potentially a mafia princess.

When Pop got back to Syracuse before his flight, he stopped at his parents' home to tell them about the engagement. It was Labor Day, 1973. Forty-seven years earlier, also Labor Day, Grampa had proposed to Gramma.

Grampa gathered from conversations with Gramma on bus rides to and from work, before they started dating, that she liked to dance. He secretly took dancing lessons and worked up the courage to ask her out. He knew a good thing in his bride the same way my father did in my mother.

This served as a profound and life-elevating moment for my dad and his position as a want to be prodigal son.

My mother was also really good with her hands, and knew how to clean copper pots with ketchup. I'm pretty sure that's what sealed the deal for my grandfather and his soon-to-be daughter-in-law.

To that end, my grandmother said to my dad, "Does Mary have any idea what she's getting into?"

Pop promised my mom that while she might not always be happy, she'd never be bored.

Upon realization that their baby would be a husband, the parents of this youngest bachelor son marched down to the chancery the next day and sold the burial plot they'd anticipated needing for him.

The wedding was before my mom's 30th birthday, because she wanted to be married in her '20s. There was no engagement ring because... well, there just wasn't. Mom purchased Pop's wedding ring, further setting the tone of bucking tradition. Her wedding ring belonged to my Great-Gramma Nellie.

Mom wore shoes three sizes too big, with athletic socks from one of my uncle's stuck in the toes, because the store didn't carry her size and she liked the style.

It was her day. It was their love.

With more than 800 guests in the church, a reality hit my mom's parents that my dad was indeed "a public person." To my mom, he was just hers.

Their song was one of the hits of 1973, a favorite of Mom's. If you asked my dad, he wouldn't recall the title. If you told my mom he didn't know, she wouldn't care.

Miracle Baby

They had filed adoption paperwork after grieving two babies: one miscarried and one stillborn son, Sean Patrick.

There was an incident involving the consumption of fresh beets one night that resulted in Mom initially thinking there was a crisis, only to hear my dad call out from the other bathroom, "It's OK! It's happening to me, too!"

My parents were on a journey together to conceive a child. It had been harrowing, with moments of humor woven throughout.

My mom's loveable OB told her that if she even thought she was pregnant, she would need to go to bed and stay there for the duration.

It happened one night at a restaurant near my parents' apartment. They had each ordered a Scotch on the rocks. It tasted awful to her. She lifted her hand to motion for the waiter and then stopped abruptly.

She knew.

And so began an expertly crafted and choreographed care plan for my mother's pregnancy with me.

The science of the day held that even though Scotch had been a flag on the field on the beginning, in the fifth month of her pregnancy Mom would need to drink red wine until the room spun. There was concern that the placenta was pulling away from her uterine wall and she would need to stay relaxed.

Her diagnosis was placenta abruptia.

Every day, Pop either ordered or prepared meals for Mom. On one occasion, she gently pulled the covers over her head in response to screams coming from the kitchen when he was left baffled and infuriated by meat that went in the broiler, but somehow never came out. The drawer under the stove contained the broiling mechanism. Mom had instructed him to place aluminum foil on the broiling pan before placing anything on top of it. When he opened the drawer, the foil got caught in the back, leaving the meat to fall down behind the broiler.

The clanging of pans hitting every surface in the kitchen and the wall drowned out his pleas of "Where's the meat?!" among other well-placed not-so-biblical language.

A strategist in politics and government and a scholar of history and literature, he was; a student of the immediate domestic cause and effect, he was not.

Everyone in Washington had been commissioned by Pop to attend to his Mary as she was with child. A baby food warming dish, fresh flowers and linen were set on the table next the bed. An aide came to assist with toileting or bathing needs while Pop was on the Hill. A tape recorder was in place so Mom could record the master's thesis she was finishing, instead of risking positional distress by writing on her back. Friends and family called, cooked and delivered well wishes. The OB extraordinaire and his nurse came to the house to monitor my progress and Mom's symptoms.

Mom talked to me every day while I was in her womb. She sang to me and read parts of her papers to me. All her sharing amused an informed me. It's why I never tire of the sound of her voice.

It's also probably why I scored 758 out of 800 on the verbal part of my SAT, with a total score of 890.

Moral of that story: red wine is helpful if you want to raise an artist, but it's not a solid move if you're hoping for a kid to manage the nuclear codes.

The day she went into labor was two and half months before my due date. It was 1978, so premature babies were up against much harsher mortality statistics than they are today.

The power went out in the building complex. Crews of electricians, firemen and EMTs were called to the scene. The initial game plan was that Mom would be lifted and lowered over the balcony of my parent's fourth floor apartment.

Mom—despite the prospect of losing another baby—remained calm and directed neighbors to keep checking the elevator as the firemen, in full uniform, attempted to make a trip with her down the stairwell instead.

Having lived through the broiler fiasco, Mom had to put my father out her mind in the midst of instructing her team to keep her in position, flat on the stretcher, parallel, not even the slightest angle.

After one flight down, a resident called to say that the elevators were up and running.

Mom was safely taken via ambulance to the hospital where she gave birth, in truth she says it was more like a bowel movement— to a 3.5 pound me, a girl.

The time honored game of "swirl the needle over the pregnant woman's belly" revealed I would most certainly be a boy. Such stock was taken in this that my parents didn't have a name for a girl.

In fairness, Pop thought Siobhan would be a beautiful name. Mom, remember, was good with her hands; she wasn't sure if there were two g's in the word plugged, so a name with that many phonetic contradictions was out of the question.

During of my 30-plus-day stay in the NICU, Mom had aggressive physical therapy to learn how to walk again, due to loss of equilibrium and muscle strength during the pregnancy.

A call came in from one of the friends present the night my parents got engaged, Millie. She wanted to know exactly what 3.5 pounds looked like. Mom, thrilled to be able to give an exacting example, told Millie I was like a Cornish hen.

Before discharging us, family, friends and staff gathered to have an impromptu naming ceremony.

My parents chose a strong name for the strong little lady they watched fight to survive.

They called me Kate.

Growing Up Miracle

My parents had been educated by nuns and priests, but they're slightly older than the generation who identify as recovering Catholics. My parents loved their faith. They lived their faith, that's what they told me.

I could not comprehend that the color of people's skin, where or how they lived or where they worshiped could be used against them. It never occurred to me not to treat everyone the same: with love and respect.

My family's faith, and any action within it, was rooted in that belief.

One of my earliest memories is standing side-by-side with homeless people, making bagged lunches and building a shelter. We weren't better people than our new friends seeking shelter or food. I can still see the face of the girl I played dolls with on the floor, while our fathers hammered nails and put up walls.

The only part of the day that was slightly odd—other than the part about my dad using a hammer without injury—was when we left. They stayed.

Another more vivid memory was me waiting for my mom when she was at the White House for a meeting. I stayed in the car. This was when you could park by the White House.

A woman sat on the wall, hitting herself periodically. People walked by and she cackled. A man stopped to give her a can of soda and a dollar bill. She stared at that dollar. She stared at the can. She repeated the sequence a few more times before eating the dollar and tossing the can.

It was explained to me later that a nearby hospital had closed, leaving many patients needing to fend for themselves on the street.

I didn't really know what that meant exactly. If I understood it correctly, Republicans and Catholics had very different views.

I grew up across the Potomac from Capitol Hill, where both of my parents were involved in legislation for equality: clean air, clean water, health care and education, to name a few of their fields of interest. Most of my friends' parents were part of Hill life, as well.

This was an era when the majority of Congress was made up of like-minded men and women to whom service was the priority.

Again, maybe I didn't totally understand that the way I do now, but Alexandria, Virginia, was not part of the machine or metropolis it is today. It was an intimate community where we knew the bank teller, the store owners, the crossing guards and the mailman. Our mayor sat in the dunk tank at the annual neighborhood fair. He returned even when he went on to work in Congress. All of my friends and I played on the same soccer team and learned piano from the same teacher. A lot of us went to the same school or the same church. Everyone came to our Christmas parties.

Those parties, I've come to learn, were legendary. Mom and I began baking cookies in October. My friends came over to frost them. She made popcorn balls for all the kids in the neighborhood. Pop did all the cleaning and prep for the bar downstairs and shoveled the walk if we had snow. He had the stereo set up to play all the old standard holiday tunes on 8-tracks or cassettes.

Our home was electric on party day, the three of us united until about two hours before people arrived. The search for shoes, a festive tie, the missing box of punch cups or a light bulb that went out were all par for the course.

Once the doorbell rang, it was like being in a holiday ballet. There was no dress code; I just remember feeling that it was all very fancy. Mom let me wear taffeta, maybe that's why.

Mom, in her early childhood genius, invented Elf Night for me. We spent every Christmas in Syracuse when I was little, which concerned me since I wasn't sure Santa would be able to find me.

A few weeks before we left to make the trek up north, we would have a special dinner, after which Pop and I would take a walk around the neighborhood to look at the lights. Meanwhile, Mom would set up a surprise under the tree. The accompanying note was a variation on the theme of, "From the Elves: Santa won't forget you in Syracuse."

Pop's position on the season was always more prophetic than commercial. He was the master of Advent.

On occasion, we invited people over to share these evenings with us in our sunroom. But usually, it was the three of us nestled in.

We had a system. I was in charge of set up and preparation on this. I would mark the Bible passages with a ribbon, select a Christmas carol to sing, open the Advent calendar, and light the candle or candles depending on the week. Mom read.

Pop pulled from both the Old and New Testaments, referencing the Pharaoh or Moses, the socio-economy of Mesopotamia, the geopolitics or feminist perspective, followed by an example in present day that tied together what our faith was all about. It was a class and Mom and I were his captivated students.

Then we'd sing together and seal the night with a kiss, all three of us leaning in, kissing at once; the time was sacred to me.

One Advent, my parents came into the sunroom to find me taking individual members of the nativity scene, including the Holy Family, and sending them to jail in a hanging planter. There must have been some show; our staple was public television.

Religion, politics and culture were one and the same in my house, all dissected around the dinner table; the extension of this was that my parents chose a less traditional path for me to partake of my first Eucharist as well.

Father Jack, a priest who knew my parents separately and together, professionally and personally, celebrated their marriage and baptized me. He was a regular at my birthday parties.

In our parish in Alexandria, a new program was offered, enabling parents to teach more at home. Mom and Pop chose to have Father Jack celebrate my first communion in Skaneateles, NY, home to some of the Franciscan Sisters of the Central New York area. Gramma Mahoney, Gramma and Grampa Speno and my uncle Gerry would be there.

Mom selected a white satin, cap-sleeve dress with a light blue sash, a color to honor the Blessed Mother. The dress size required me to somewhat compromise my breathing. I couldn't bend or reach. I picked out a wreath of tiny roses woven in babies' breath to wear in my hair and my white patent buckle shoes were an obvious choice. I carried a small white missalette with rosary beads belonging to my great-grandmother. Father Jack's scarf had all the animals from Noah's Ark in pockets that I could take out and play with. I'm sure I knew the word for sacred vestments, but I didn't overthink it. We were both dressed up for the occasion.

The priest was not someone more important on this day than any other day. He mattered all the time. He was family.

I think my eyes have always seen relationship first, regulations second.

Rita O'Malley

On a bright and beautiful April day, Pop said with all the gentility of a wrecking ball, "You will go and you will like it!"

Ireland was my parents' dream, not mine. Pop was asked to set up the first American Government program at the collegiate level in Ireland. Mom intended to create educational opportunities for teen mothers.

I had polished trophies from soccer that clearly stated it was a local team. Why would I break my winning streak? The pizza place we went to was the best in the world. It said so on the menu. Did they even have pizza in Ireland? I was cantor in the church choir. My voice was an integral part of our Sunday program! My house was the only home I'd ever need; a home was about four walls when I was 12. And my friends! I had a select group of friends who knew which boys I like-liked, my favorite songs and my favorite oversized on trend sweater.

Leaving this would be the end of life, as I knew life to be. I hatched several plans to prevent this uprooting.

Abby, one of my first friends ever, helped me hang red tablecloths over the Open House signs. Thanks to the Christmas parties, we had cloths in several sizes and shapes that worked on various signs around the block. The realtor expressed to my parents the challenges of selling or renting a house without proper signage. Mom thoughtfully countered that I was "working through some things."

My friend Sarah offered her garage for me to live in. She couldn't offer the house without talking to her parents, and it was evident that the parents were plotting against us. Cara figured we could have a fundraiser, maybe even use some outtakes from our radio show. As we assessed the various moving parts of our operation, things started to unravel. There wasn't plumbing in Sarah's garage... or heat... or a bed.

Our radio show probably couldn't help me fund a lemonade stand, let alone parochial school tuition. Also, it was actually just us screaming '90s ballads in rounds, occasionally reading passages from young adult books into a cassette player. We did take callers, but it was primarily from her dog, Ziggy.

I was told the house would be rented. They—the people who would be living in my home—came to do what they called a "walk through." The woman wore hot pink and tangerine. Her scrunchie matched her socks perfectly. I wanted to like her but she was an evil imposter.

The man with her travelled up the stairs and to the landing in the house. One of the steps creaked. That was the step my friend Katie and I sprung from when we performed show tunes. Pop explained that was his security system. I was aghast. He was far too cavalier about sharing our home invasion secrets. I had to take things into my own hands. I had to play the only child card.

The next day, I threw a bunch of my stuffed animals out the window. I crawled under my bed. My parents would see the animals on the lawn, so I thought, and they might think I had jumped and run away. This would bring them to their senses.

I should have known then that I would end up in drama, not an engineering program. If I had jumped, the fall from my window could have killed me—or at the very least, left me with multiple broken bones—hindering my escape from the yard.

By August, the boxes were stacked up in air cargo at the airport. Between fits of sobbing, I wrote my friends epic letters on tear-stained college-ruled paper and filed them in my super secure binder. We had made promises never to forget each other, no matter what.

Those hip preteen boutiques saw me coming when they offered the best friends necklaces that resembled broken hearts. I bought out the store, I think. I was 12; everyone I knew was my best friend. How could I move a million miles away without leaving a token of our friendships? I mean, I was going to die as a result of this move, anyway. They should have something to remember me by, right?

Autumn of 1990 was marked by collective green necks from cheap jewelry. I was unaware the role consumerism played in our American culture.

Our refrigerator in Limerick was slightly larger than my backpack. Our milk man—yes, we had a milk man—was concerned that we ordered skim milk, and wanted to know if it was a misprint on the form, since none of us looked to have a heart condition. The thought that we would drink skim by choice baffled him. The shop down the road carried one kind of toothpaste, several packages of cookies—biscuits, they were called—the newspapers, and other sweets or incendiaries, but no more than one or two of each item.

All students wore uniforms and rode public transportation to school. That part was OK, since my parents bought a robin's egg blue sedan. Bought might be a strong word. It was like they found it somewhere. The front seat could lift off the floor and be turned around to face the back. No problem, as long as you placed your foot over the floor when it rained, so that water from the road wouldn't come up through the rusted-out holes.

This was the backdrop for my new life. It was not quite so terrifying or dramatic. It was rather enticing. With each encounter, I was less convinced of my imminent death. There was way too much exploring to do.

One of my neighbors was in charge of opening the gates for the train on our road. Her daughters were among my new acquaintance group in the neighborhood. They used to love to say, "Myy nayme is Kayte Mahoneee and Eye'm from Amerrica." I could handle that since they were in awe of my ability to expertly roll French cuffs on my USA-made acid wash jeans, complete with front pleats at the waist.

On the weekends, between trains, my new gal pals and I followed the tracks a few miles to a shop called O'Reilly's. Behind the shop, there was a small building. Inside, we talked about our favorite bands and made up dance routines to songs on the jukebox, an actual jukebox.

It wasn't the same as the choreography I'd mastered alongside my self-proclaimed backup dancer friends back in Alexandria. We had worked mainly with one or two cassettes. Regardless, I was finding my rhythm with these girls. Occasionally we played pool; mostly we watched the boys.

My first kiss was at a disco, what I would have called a school dance. I wore a black mock turtleneck sweater, made in the US, adorned with a multicolored swirl pattern. I'm pretty sure I donned a red satin headband with a bow. I wore that everywhere.

If you're thinking that look must have been spectacular, you'd be correct.

The boy's name was Paul. He seemed nice for someone I'd never met in my life. My new friend and strangers alike circled us and yelled things like, "Kiss the American!"

It was over no sooner than it began, and everyone in the hall cheered. It had been a bet or an initiation of some kind—maybe for each of us? I couldn't wait to get home and write in my diary that my sweater would be renamed "the sweater I kissed Paul in" and document that I had attended a disco when I lived in Ireland.

Embarrassment was fleeting. I wondered if anyone would be able to tell when they looked at me, like when I got my first bra; I did think I looked a bit taller afterward. All these moments were on par with sacraments for me at that tender age.

Catholic kids my age in Ireland—and there were many of them—had already made their confirmation (a Catholic rite of passage). My parents decided I would join the class of students a year younger than me; however, that group was too far along in the curriculum for me to catch up.

So, true to form, my parents set up a one-on-one arrangement with me and our parish priest. I wasn't sure what to expect, but I knew not to wear the sweater the boy at the disco kissed me in when I met him.

Mom had the tea made, fresh peat thrown on the fire and the Bible was all set up in the den for us to dissect like we would at home with Father Jack. The priest came in the house. He had a very thick accent. I had begun to decipher a handful of dialects, yet I swore this man kept calling me Rita O'Malley. We'd adjusted to people calling us O'Mahony. This was not that.

Our seeming inability to connect on my name should have been a clue to the overall language barrier we had in regards to our faith in action. Catholicism in Ireland in the early '90s was akin to the '40s or '50s in the States. Divorce was only newly legal when we moved there. Judgment was swift; guilt was expected. Free will was American.

My independent study essay on my relationship with Jesus—the one where I said Jesus was like an alien—didn't go over very well.

I remember Mom and I waiting in the kitchen while Pop and Father spoke behind closed doors. I don't know if there was an indulgence transfer or what, but when they appeared in the hall, I had been cleared to meet the bishop and receive the sacrament of Confirmation.

Way to go, Rita! I mean, me.

What was sacred was that it was the day my country cousins met my city cousins for the first time. They'd lived only a few miles from one another in Ireland for generations. Mom had invited them and they all came; one family from a thatched cottage on a peat bog, the other from a two-story house in the city.

Even now, my heart swells when I think of the communion in our kitchen.

We made my grandmother's chocolate cake. The little ones loved the frosting. There was a fullness in our home that day. I did call it a home. It had nothing to do with the walls at all.

Over the course of the next academic year and a half, we hosted holiday and less calendar-worthy parties that brought together other people who'd lived down the road from one another for years and had never met.

I went to two different schools, performed in one stage production, learned how to ride horses and started the first girls' soccer team, which my mom coached.

Our home whether in our hearts or connected to our driveway was a gathering place for all. The door was always open. I remember lots of laughter-cackling, howling, raucous, joyous laughter.

When it came time to leave, I was devastated. The thought of leaving these people, my best friends, overwhelmed me. I cried the whole way back over the ocean; between sobs, I wrote letters of intent on my college-ruled paper and filed them in my super secure binder. I promised to return the following summer.

My illness changed that itinerary.

It was the summer of 1996 that I got back to the lads in Limerick. I was in a wheel chair, with leg braces. At some point in between, I had worn the sweater I kissed Paul in for a portrait gallery glamour shot, and was able to hand out wallet-sized photos to my friends who'd kept me current through letters.

I navigated the old road with new legs and renewed perspective. I learned how to ride a bike for the first time, again. Doctors told me I wouldn't be able to maneuver that. Apparently, I defied medical expectations overseas, too.

Mom and I went home to Ireland again after Pop died. They had widened the roads and now sold more kinds of toothpaste. Still, the simplicity of a cup of tea or a pint welcomed us back as if we'd never left.

One evening, my friends and I arrived in a pub around half past ten. The place was aglow. People from town trickled in. Instrument by instrument, music began to play. It was unclear whether or not the musicians knew one another; it didn't matter.

We sat across from one another, enjoying fresh pints of beer and nips of whiskey. Our eyes met in between songs, the flickering lights like a film reel that took us back in time. My friends for over 25 years, ones with whom I could have whole conversations that required no words.

On that night, we were all chatter. Between us, we'd had job changes, marriage and kids, learned to drive, gone to college, lost a parent and had a Vatican-documented miracle.

Each milestone was on the level with the others; there had been so much life lived as individuals over those 17 years since I'd last wheeled back into their lives.

In a breath, a blink—we swooned in nostalgia reliving ages 11, 12 and 13. Any talk around the miracle was fleeting. The reality was that had we stayed in Ireland, I would have most certainly died. And sure, there was no need to wax extemporaneous on all that. We joked we'd send all inquiries to Rita O'Malley.

Side Bar

Toward the end of our second year in Ireland, Pop asked Mom if she thought it would be okay if he had a drink. He'd been sober since they found out she was pregnant with me.

I don't think either of them in that moment realized he was asking for permission.

Not too long after that, everything I knew to be true about my parents changed. I couldn't express it at the time, but this was the beginning of my awareness that my parents were people.

My scholarly, charismatic, reliable Pop—who had an infinite capacity for responsibility, love and wit—faded away. He was replaced by an angry, reactionary, easily-wounded, mean man who on all accounts looked the same, yet bore no resemblance.

In my recollection, Mom was never around, nor was she aware of the severity of the situation. Her seeming passive negligence incensed me. It was like we weren't living in the same house. Where was she to help me battle him as he tore through the house in pursuit of quenching this unquenchable thirst?

I clung to every shred of power I thought I possessed at 13. I verbally and physically fought him with everything I had. Only once did he hit me so hard that it lifted me off the ground, sending me into a wall.

I have no sense memory of the actual hit.

I was aware I was sliding down the wall. Everything felt simultaneously fast and slow. Like a hunted, captured animal, I went numb, no longer thinking his behavior wasn't right, good or normal. Instead, in quiet defeat, I accepted it as familiar and routine. But, it wasn't that routine either. Up until that point, my skin was thickened only for the verbal lashings.

He spilled his drink with that last slap. Enraged by the mess, he launched the glass toward me. It missed, and shattered onto the floor. I dutifully cleaned up and left no visible trace of the event.

My mother never showed up that night.

Loving someone in the throes of addiction is a series of decisions made in a very delicate balance.

Every feeling that every person has must be acknowledged and validated; yet regardless of feelings, somewhat immediate action is imperative in order to move toward an existence of health, stability and security. It's not always clear how to proceed.

Lucky for us, I got cancer.

My diagnosis shook my parents to their very core. In truth, I was so close to shattered, cancer didn't scare me. Instead, it was a burden that would surely destroy them. If I had any feeling other than being overwhelmed, it was guilt about that.

We didn't have any money or insurance or home. I didn't want to be the reason our family dissolved.

While we acted as a unit for most of my young life, in the early days of my diagnosis, we were three separate individuals, three self-centered survivors.

Pop—up against his disease—was in his most vulnerable state. It defied logic, reason, history and all his dreams for the future. It was exhausting, frustrating and depleting—again for everyone involved, including him. He tried to quit like before; he made pacts with and promises to God, but the disease had progressed.

Mom was able to call upon his former contacts, and secure him a place on the detox floor.

He was in treatment when I started chemo.

At first, as his chemical makeup regulated itself, he was quick to blame my mother for ruining our family. I was angry with her for not helping me stand up to him in Ireland, so part of me aligned with him.

Still, I wanted him to be grateful to her for getting him the help he couldn't get on his own.

I credit the nurses for creating the time and space for us to process all this. They let me ride in the food service elevators to the detox floor so I could see Pop. He wasn't supposed to have visitors, and I wasn't supposed to travel all over the hospital with a compromised immune system. They knew we needed each other to get through this. They put chocolates on the pillow and found empty beds where Mom could rest.

Pop's and my initial discharges from the hospital were around the same time. He packed a bag and got ready to go to an inpatient rehab facility. I was so incredibly conflicted. I had been hurled into a very adult set of circumstances. I desperately wanted him to go and to stay.

I put Brown Bear in Pop's bag to take with him. He gave me his bunny from when he was a child. My grandmother still had it in the cedar chest. It was kind of her to get it for me; though not as thoughtful was her comment, "I've just never known anyone who had a problem with alcohol." That all but mortally wounded my father who was hanging by a thread anyway.

It was her truth that no one she'd ever known was an alcoholic, and it was painfully comical given the long line of people in our family who'd been described to me as ones who "liked the 'sauce.'"

I think the family was preoccupied with the idea of saving Pop's career, image or relationship with friends and family. Each had their merits, but the true goal of saving his life sadly got lost in all the noise.

Pop's family wasn't equipped with the language to navigate the disease. Like so many other Irish Catholics, they were raised to pray away the problems and keep matters private. Going to a rehab facility meant letting out the secret that something was wrong, sinful even. The little boy who knew all the presidents bore the weight of a lifetime of imperfections and sadly carried the guilt of several generations with him to detox.

At the same time, his marriage was a little shaky and his daughter was terminally ill. His choice to heal was overshadowed by many people's desire to keep up appearances.

I can still feel the three of us in the parking lot of the rehab center, hugging all together—like our Advent wreath kiss.

When I went into Critical Care, Pop wasn't even halfway through his program. Many people—friends and family—continued to judge him harshly. They viewed his absence as failure to be of service and support to his wife or some type of abandonment. Similar judgment revisited us years later when his diagnosis of primary liver cancer came. There was talk of pay back and other wasteful shaming language Mom and I had no use for.

Blame should never be a reason not to accept, especially if it's at the expense of facts.

When I was in ICU, Mom knew where Pop was; she knew he was safe. She knew he was where he was supposed to be. And more importantly, she knew she was better equipped to handle my illness. Why would she want to manage two patients in crisis? Mom continued to love the John Mahoney she fell for back in that smoke-filled bar so many years ago. She felt strongly that steps had to be taken to provide methodical and safe long-term measures: therapeutic, psychological, medical, emotional and physical supports.

You'll never convince me that he wasn't by my side every moment, despite being miles away, or that my mother was mad at him for taking care of himself so that he could care for us.

Disease doesn't know it is Christmas or New Year's or your birthday. Regardless of holidays, levels of previous expectations or any quick fix that might seem to work in the interest of time, anything less than total acceptance, is a complete disservice to the patient.

When I came out of my coma, my parents were there. They were still married. To me, the chance to continue to be a family was the real miracle.

I believe Mother Marianne chose all three of us to be vehicles for recovery. None of us had jobs. He couldn't drink, I couldn't walk and Mom had been awake for about four months. If there was ever a poster family for starting anew, it was us!

Anyone recovering from any disease tends to go into fight mode, with the ideal of getting back to where they were; in their mind, that's the sign they are okay. In retrospect however, we learn that we are changed and cannot go back. We can only go forward. And in most cases, we don't want to go all the way back, because we are no longer the person we were going into the fight. Fight doesn't always have a negative connotation. A fight for joy is as much of a battle as a fight against disease.

Days before Pop died—before the funeral with the Baptist choir, the Lutheran minister, the Rabbi, the Catholic Bishop, the gay lector, the sign language interpreter, Hispanic, Irish, Latin and gospel songs and the merry band of theologians in between— before Mom and I greeted 1,600 plus people at the wake, I sat at home with my head resting on Pop as he lay in the hospital bed. I didn't want to speak because I didn't want to disturb him. In my head, I asked Mother to let me know everything would be okay.

Pop shifted his body and opened his eyes, with a confused expression. He turned to face me and said, "I just want you to know everything is going to be okay." He gently closed his eyes and put his head back on the pillow.

In the face of one of the hardest losses I've ever had to bear, okay never looked so clear.

Act II
The Mis-Fit Miracle

"I may be a miracle. But I'm also a person."

That Time My Life Changed Overnight

You are age 14. What does it look like? Where do you live? What have you already experienced? Have you been truly terrified? Totally happy? Have you known love?

When I was 14, I'd gone to five schools in five years, moved from my childhood home—a place so perfect I didn't know why anyone would ever want to leave it—across the ocean to Ireland.

I had been a soccer phenom, a cantor in the church choir, a guest pianist with the Alexandria Symphony, multiple characters in multiple theatrical productions and a friend. Yes, I was an only child, but my friendships ran deep and familial.

It was a couple months after my 14th birthday. We were back from Ireland, with the intention to move back to our home in Alexandria, where my idyllic life would resume. My parents and I were on Lake Ontario renting a cottage—as we had every summer of my life, and every summer of theirs, too, before they were grownups or married or parents.

My best friend Abby came up to visit. We splashed in the waves, searched for shells on the sand, got tan and burned, rode bikes, talked about boys and listened to girl anthems and boy bands on my lavender shoulder-strap adorned cassette player. I think it took eight D batteries. It was no joke.

Abby and I had been classmates, teammates, neighbors and friends since we were 2. In first grade, a new girl came to our school, and I told our teacher that she had stolen my best friend. I was the dramatic one in the friendship.

Abby would stand with me outside a bar after my dad's funeral telling me that we were in a club now. Her dad died after our senior year in college. We've shared a lot of life.

In 1992, at age 14, we were just best friends hangin' out on the beach.

I didn't feel well. That's such a generic thing to say, but it was just that. I was tired, despite sound sleep accompanied by fresh air; cold, regardless of the fact that it was August and 90 degrees; sick to my stomach, though I hadn't eaten anything.

We dropped Abby off at the airport to go back to Virginia, and my mom drove me into Syracuse to my grandparents' doctor. I don't remember much, but I know they drew lots of blood, took my temperature and sent me home to monitor symptoms, while we waited for results on what was presumed to be a smoldering appendix.

Home: let me be clear, it was not my home. It was my dad's mother's house. I adored her. We were friends. She and my mom were soulmates. But it wasn't my room or my house or my street or my neighborhood.

What I remember next could have filled either a couple hours or a couple days. I can see the registration window of the Emergency Room at the hospital. I was in a wheelchair, in and out of consciousness. I was vomiting in the bathroom, because I can still feel how cold the tile floor was on my face. What came out of me was like a mixture of grass and gravel. It was dark and gritty.

I know my mom was there. I think my dad was there.

At some point, my mom's father walked in. I could hear the pacing of a cane and penny loafers on the floor before the curtain around my bed was pulled back.

"What the Hell are you doing here?"

Again, he could have stayed a minute or an hour; everything was happening so fast.

Cut to me in a bed on a medical floor beyond the ER. I guess I'd been admitted. I'm pretty sure my bed was by the door, not the window, and I don't think I had a roommate. A man in a white coat came to the side of my bed.

"Hi. I'm from Oncology."

"Hi. I'm from Virginia."

I thought we were just saying where we were from.

I looked to the foot of my bed where my parents stood. Pop's eyes were red. The only time I'd ever seen him cry was when his father died. It was the first time I'd seen him cry and I was 5. This time around, the redness was one of two things: fear and sadness related to my situation, or potentially residual effects from his return to "the sauce."

You should realize that at no point was I attached to my fear or my illness or any of the experience. It was all totally overwhelming and all at once. Was my dad sober? Was my mom nearby? What is oncology? I think I threw up on my shoes. Where are my underpants? I miss my dog. All of it was of equal importance, which is what 14 is, isn't it? It's what life is, too; as we grow, we put parameters on what we think it is we're allowed to feel and when.

I don't remember going down for surgery or even what it was exactly that was going to happen while I was in surgery. I'd had a procedure when I was 9 to stitch a skin thing on my arm. I remember they told me I couldn't wear underwear on the table and I thought that was not alright; so I kept mine on—white cotton with little purple flower buds on them. This time, I came and went through the OR with only the gown and Brown Bear.

A stage 4 malignant germ cell ovarian tumor—the size of a basketball—was removed from my abdomen. How could we not see a giant tumor in my belly, you ask? Well, I was what they called "big-boned" as a child, which is the nice way of saying, "There's a chance you escaped from your yak herd, but will be raised by these nice people who, oddly enough, you look like." Also, the tumor was pressed inward against my back.

I remember when the staples came out. I don't remember it hurting. It must have. The staples were thick, shiny surgical steel. There were about 27 of them holding my scar, a scar which ran from just above my belly button all the way down between my legs to my private parts. I was 14.

I wasn't well-versed in my lady business just yet. I'd only had one period. Remember what I said: all new, and all at once.

There was no internet to research reviews or treatment options. My doctor had successfully removed the tumor with the latest technology of the day, a machine equivalent to a vacuum cleaner. My left ovary and tube were removed as well.

How many other parts of me would be removed or reshuffled until I came crashing down?

The chemo protocol was intense; I was one of only about a thousand people nationally with this germ cell and ovarian cancer diagnosis. I was set up for six sessions, or courses—I don't remember what we were calling it. It required me to be in the hospital for seven to10 days, and it would be administered through an IV. There were no infusion centers then and pills weren't part of my treatment, aside from managing side effects such as nausea and dry mouth.

Pop, in his mastery of running campaigns, and Mom, the beacon of early childhood education, were a force putting together my immediate care plan.

We had no insurance. So my dad talked to lots of people and secured me a place in the hospital.

We had no home. So my grandmother opened her doors and the movers brought a handful of boxes.

We couldn't take care of my dog. She had been at my godmother's in Pennsylvania while we were in Ireland; due to quarantine regulations, she would stay put a little longer.

We had no income. So my parents sold our house in Virginia, and Pop began searching for any work available. My mom's place would be full time by my side in the hospital.

Take note: anyone who has ever been a caregiver knows that full-time medical care for a family member is 24/7. Training for Olympic Gold might be a distant second in terms of the endurance that's required and the sacrifices that are necessary.

I didn't have a school. After several interviews with several schools, we somewhat agreed on a Catholic school and a tutor to help me stay on top of my course load while in treatment.

No friends, no dog, no home, no school, no church choir, no piano and no soccer team. And after a couple chemo cycles, no hair.

I'm not going to tell you that it was all awful. We had a tremendous support network of friends, family, spiritual and medical practitioners, some of whom you'll get to know here. And we laughed a lot. But in those first few days, I felt nothing and everything all the time.

Hello, My Name Is Cancer, But You Can Call Me Miracle

I don't believe I've ever met anyone who claimed to have loved high school. I'm not sure I've met anyone who even truly liked it. I think we project our feelings of ourselves onto this thing called high school and justify behaviors after the fact.

I went to a Catholic high school.

There are some archaic rules in the church surrounding human feelings, due to what I think is a long history of disconnects where hormones are concerned. There's anxiety, anticipation, maybe some perspiration.

To my knowledge, most of my classmates had known each other since birth or at least kindergarten. I was friends with one kid. He was my summer friend; his parents and my parents all knew each other in their youth, so we visited and played mini golf once every summer.

I didn't have the luxury of introducing myself the first day of school, because I was in chemo the first week of classes. That was before infusion centers or video conference calls, before the culture dictated that cancer and life didn't need to mutually exclusive.

By the time I arrived to school, my identity had been secured. It appeared my stats were that I had cancer and wasn't from the area, so everyone needed to feel bad for me, pray for me and be nice to me. The kids would have done that anyway; but knowing that someone was lording over them, mandating their goodness, made me uneasy. Who was being nice to me because we were all peers, and who was doing what they were told? That thinking didn't set me up for success.

It's like if someone tells you that you should feel good because they paid you a compliment; it sort of negates the compliment. There was so much Jesus talk; it seemed to come at the expense of basic exchanges and pleasantries. I didn't know that some of my classmates had lost parents or siblings or had illnesses of their own. I actually didn't know I was allowed to inquire. Because of my treatments, my schedule was inconsistent. My interactions were more with the grownups and I let their estimation of my existence become my narrative. I started building walls up without even realizing I was doing it.

The more side effects I suffered from, the more school I missed. The more school I missed, the further behind I fell in classes and social order. The further I fell, the harder it was to share my happy, healthy self. Whether I was in the hospital or at home, I sobbed to my parents. I blamed everything on our move from Virginia to Ireland. In my mind, if we had never done that, this chain of events would never have occurred.

On the days I did go to school, there were celebrations and fundraisers on my behalf. My entire life was so up in the air, I resented the fact that people I didn't know used me to break a stupid dress code rule and then expected me to be effusive with my gratitude. I was so lost and so very lonely. When I used to say I hated high school, it was really because I hated myself. My illness and this overhanging assessment that cancer was a determining factor in my overall makeup as a young woman destroyed my independence, structure, and capacity to believe I was included— the normal desires for a young person.

Every time someone said they were praying for me, I pursed my lips and nodded as if to say thank you. But I wanted to scream, "DON'T PRAY FOR ME. GET TO KNOW ME. IT'S THE SAME THING." The flip side of that was if someone did ask me to go to their house or a game, I didn't have the energy all the time, because I had cancer. It was a vicious cycle of trying to deny and accept my reality. Prior to my diagnosis, prior to being a student in a Catholic school, I had really loved being a Catholic, which is what made the miracle piece of the puzzle all the more frustrating. I felt like an outcast.

After my miraculous recovery, I still had to attend school. Granted, it was for an hour or so in between therapy appointments in April, and the last time I'd been in a classroom it had been October. I missed some academic and life skills. My hair was coming back in, so no obvious out of dress code hat for me. But I was in a wheel chair, had leg braces, and my voice was barely a whisper because of the intubation and vocal chord scarring. On top of that, my fine motor skills were compromised, which affected test and note taking. My large muscle groups were weak, so I couldn't perform in even the most basic of gym class activities.

Still, the most difficult obstacle for me was grappling with the fact that my teachers and classmates had first-hand knowledge of my time in ICU and I had no memory at all. They had received daily updates while I was in the hospital. I, on the other hand, woke up from a coma having no idea how seriously ill I had been, only struggling to regain function in every cell in my body from head to toe. Wheeling into school to whispers of "She's the one we prayed for" drove my resentment deeper.

I just wanted to be Kate Mahoney. Why couldn't anyone get that? In fact, they did; but I was the little girl they prayed for, and they were excited about that more than anything else. Who could really blame them? I guess I get that now.

The truth is my anger dissipated with every recovery milestone I hit, though I opted to go back to school in Virginia to mark the occasions. Mind you, I was not enrolled in school in Virginia, I just went there when my school was on break and sat in classes, study halls and in the cafeteria, so I could be with my friends. Looking back, I'd made building relationships with new people far more difficult for myself. My parents were just so happy I was alive, that they facilitated my travel however they could for a couple years. But my mom really did want me to have an authentic high school experience before graduation.

So, naturally, she set up my prom date. Really? Yes! (Awesome).

His name was Brian. He was actually a student at another school, but friends with my summer friend and classmate, Christian. Christian called Brian, then Christian's mom called Brian's mom, then Brian's mom called my mom, then my mom called Christian's mom, and finally Brian called me, to ask me to my own prom. No, that wasn't weird at all.

The mothers were all a flutter on this plan. Again, I couldn't get out of my own way to see what a powerful act of love and solidarity this was for my mom after all she'd been through. I fought her at almost every turn.

She wanted me to have my dress made. I selected a heavy, black crepe fabric and a floor-length, long-sleeve, crew-neck style. It was beautifully made, but I looked like I was wearing a casket liner. I didn't have the balance or coordination to wear heels, and I didn't want anyone to see my flats. The dialysis scar on my arm embarrassed me, so I wanted my arms covered. My hair was newly mine again and I had sworn I wouldn't put product in it or do anything to it. As a result, I looked like I'd stood in water and tried to play music on a fuse box.

Brian pulled up to the house in a car that appeared to only have three tires, and when he got out, he was limping. There had been multiple calamities at his house which involved a lawn mower, his dad's good car and a trip to the ER, a tennis racket and a broken window, and tweezers and a cigarette lighter.

Mom and Pop's smiles reached from one side of our living room to the other while Brian pinned on my corsage (he totally grazed my boob). Off we went to dinner and the big dance. We had our obligatory photo and picked up our festive, commemorative glass... and didn't see each other again until Christian got married nearly 10 years later. We never danced at the prom, but we did at the wedding.

Everything fades and softens with time.

The reality is that I do have very close friends from high school. I had more time getting to know them than I allowed for coming to terms with my own predicament. Each time we reconnect, I get another glimpse into a life that was not entirely or accurately mine. To most of my classmates, I wasn't the little girl they prayed for; I was Kate Mahoney, just a girl they went to school with. Apparently I fell for the hype of my miracle, too. In their eyes I was what I wanted to be all along.

Coming full circle in a sense, I was invited and agreed to deliver the commencement address at my high school, 18 years after I graduated.

The benefit of the years is that in a circle, such as the one of Catholic schools, I had essentially accepted that I was being asked to speak because of what happened to me, and only partially because of who I was. Or so I thought.

I asked the administration if I could meet with the students before the ceremony, to get to know them, and we agreed on a time a couple months before graduation. I sat in the classroom where I took my first history class that first week of school in

September 1992. I had known maybe two people, and my hair had begun to fall out because I was in the middle of a chemo session.

The introduction included such phrases like, "It's an honor for us…"

I not comfortable with that. Not that it isn't true or in any way disingenuous, but as I explained to the students, if it was an honor to meet me, then it was an honor for me to meet them.

There was a collective breath on the part of the teachers when I said that no questions were off limits. A young man raised his hand.

"Do you like blueberries?"

"I DO!" I replied, and we talked about fruit for a minute or two.

Another hand went up: "Do you like ice cream?"

"What flavor?" The snack bar inquiry went on for a bit, and as the shoulders of everyone in the room relaxed, another hand went up.

"Were you afraid when you thought you would die?"

I spent the whole day in that room with students. We were getting to know one another. Occasionally, one of my former teachers would pop in to say hello. Every kid from seventh to twelfth grade came in with questions, ranging from innocent and seemingly unrelated to profound.

I love high school.

No, I Didn't See A Bright Light

I have no memory of my time in the intensive care unit. If I was in a tunnel, I didn't know it. This is my version of my history as told to me by people with varying perspectives and perceptions at the time of my crisis. There is plenty of documentation in medical journals and Vatican records that speak to exacting facts and figures. This part of my story is a reflection of such documentation. I believe what I am telling you to be the truth.

I am told I cried out that my back hurt. I directed my mother to press on my back repeating to her, "Press harder! You can't hurt me."

There was a blockage to my portal vein. I was in renal and hepatic failure. Ascites was building up; my body literally unable to rid itself of fluid. Due to my pain and labored breathing, clear scans were attempted but could not be obtained; instead I was sent immediately from radiology to special procedures for a paracentesis in which 4 liters of fluid were drained from my belly. I then began to bleed internally.

Mom stood outside the procedure room. She could hear me scream, "I'm falling! I'm falling…"

I was in cardiac arrest for 25 minutes.

As they ran down the hallway alongside my gurney, my oncologist handed my chart to the head of the intensive care unit and said to my mother, "This is Kate's doctor now."

My cancer protocol halted and focus shifted to systemic crisis care.

Upon my arrival in the ICU, my oxygen sats had plummeted, my hematocrit was 10. According to the mortality assessment charts at the time of admission, there was a less than two percent chance I would survive. I was not yet at my sickest.

My soft tissue was like butter that had been left out in a warm room, which made the emergency intubation and all other surgical procedures that much more challenging. I was edematous. Subcutaneous fluid continued to build, affecting all my organs and system functions. In what could have been overnight, I went from

132 to 212 pounds. My right lung collapsed, requiring a chest tube to be inserted.

Under the supervision of at least 17 specialists and the care of round-the-clock nurses, I lay in a medically-induced coma of sorts; I was given amnesiacs and sedation which allowed me to stay still, aware of what was happening as it was happening, but with no capacity to resist or memory after the fact.

I was the face of multisystem organ failure.

Meanwhile, Back At The Miracle Factory

Sister Mary Laurence—a nun charged with the cause of canonization for a deceased sister by the name of Mother Marianne Cope—was having a holiday meal with her cousins, Jim and Rita, and Rita's cousin, Sister Rose, a nun in the same order.

Jim had been my dad's boss for many years on Capitol Hill. Rita took me for my very first ice cream cone when I was a toddler. We were Irish Catholic Democratic family.

Jim shared over dinner that I was in the intensive care unit and it did not look good. The Sisters asked if my parents would be open to praying to Mother Marianne, specifically, to ask that she intercede in my recovery.

Though I was unaware at the time, Mother Marianne was a woman who embodied devotion to God and medical administrative expertise. The Sisters weren't offering a rookie.

If you've ever been connected to someone in a medical crisis, you know that it's not unheard of for loved ones to pray for healing, life and return to normalcy—all of it. My parents, family and friends who prayed were doing just that. Those with a less institutionally-based belief system also gave what they could in support and love.

After meeting with the Sisters, a request was shared with anyone who inquired—in the hospital and beyond—that prayer intentions on my behalf should be addressed to Mother Marianne Cope, specifically asking her to posthumously intercede in my recovery.

Compared to today's methods of communication and notification, this process was antiquated.

Mom called from the hospital pay phone or line at the nurses' station and spoke with Mary Laurence hourly to request specific prayers, depending on my status or required procedures. One call might have been for platelets, another for my liver. I was jaundiced for quite some time. Yet another might have been for a procedure in which I was receiving dialysis or a shunt, and still more addressing infection control or other ongoing concerns.

Sister, on the other end of the phone, handwrote notes detailing the requests, and walked down the long hallways of the convent to place them on the bulletin boards in and around the elevators. At any given time, anyone coming and going from the convent would see these notes; many of them took out paper of their own and in turn copied the requests to take with them where they were going in their day.

Family members, friends, colleagues and members of the hospital associated with my care also spread the word in their respective communities.

The circles grew and grew. People who had never even met me or my parents joined people who greatly respected and loved us. Letters came from all over the country with words of support and hope. It was a nondenominational international effort; a Catholic-origin, grassroots movement spanning demographics, defying logic and breaking barriers.

At no time were doctors asked to remove themselves from their more immediate or hands-on careplan, though there were times in which monitoring was the only viable course of action. They deserve undying gratitude for their skill, dedication, and communication, given all the compromising elements within my ever-changing status.

There were those who questioned and doubted the persistence of care or the presence of God. For me, this is not a story about religion in the absence of science or vice versa; it's about belief that everyone has a place.

Slowly, sometimes unremarkably, each time an organ or system function was prayed for, it returned to a functioning degree, which enabled doctors to resume a more active role. When my breathing tube was removed, I had trouble supporting sound, due in part to abraded vocal tissues and weakened muscles and lungs. My body had atrophied, rendering me unable to control or sustain movement in my head or extremities. I had nerve damage in my feet and hands, fine motor deficits, scars and wounds. There were tubes coming out of every part of me.

I remember the glare of the florescent lights on the ceiling, blocking the details of peoples' faces walking beside me, hovering over me as we rolled away and towards places equally unknown.

Even now, I'm gripped somewhat by the fear of that time.

Tears come again at the memory of them streaming down my face, unaccompanied by loud cries; coming down off so many drugs, I couldn't make them. Helpless and terrified, I was unable to fight or flee.

My discharge papers stated my recovery could not be explained medically.

I needed far more than that to be explained to me.

The Relic

When Sister Mary Laurence initially came to the hospital, she brought with her a piece of a bookmark belonging to Mother Marianne. In the Church, an item like this is called a relic. Think of it as a trinket or token belonging to someone who is a great distance from you, but whom you need to feel close to, connect with, and rely on in times of unrest.

The relic was placed on me in the Intensive Care Unit in conjunction with prayers said directly to Mother. Many people felt the relic was the thing that cured me. The relic has great significance.

My story is about prayer, too. It's not the tangible, rather the belief.

The first memory I have of Sister Mary Laurence or said relic was when I was back up on the oncology floor, after ICU and after progressive care.

This woman, dressed as a nun, floated in with no words, touched my head with a piece of saran wrap—the relic—and floated away. I lay frozen, still unable to manipulate my body or words to participate in this exchange. A few minutes later, Mom came in. With all the breath I had I said to her, "Who was that?!"

"Oh. That was Sister Mary Laurence, with a relic from Mother Marianne. It's all part of your miracle." She beamed.

I was in total disbelief. There hadn't been a miracle. I was unable to walk or talk, hold my own head up, go to the bathroom or eat without a team of people guiding me. The only reason I was alive was because of the doctors. Case closed.

Little did I know; it was case just opening…

I wanted no part of the relic. To be clear, I wanted no part of any of it. But once outside the hospital, people wanted to see the relic, know about the relic and ask me how it felt to be touched by the relic. It was gross and creepy, that's how! The only relic I wanted was Brown Bear. He had been with me through everything, and he tied me to what I knew to be my life and my history.

It wasn't until I came back to Syracuse at age 25 that my relic or my relationship with Mother Marianne became important to me.

I sat in the classroom up on my first day of Home Health Aide training. The lights went out and the projector came on. There on the wall in front of me was this photo depicting the exact same image as my little card on which the bookmark thread belonging to Mother Marianne was attached.

I looked around the room, certain a joke was being played on me. When I returned home, I asked Mom to get the relic out; that's really when my parents and I talked about the whole story from the beginning. I still wasn't ready to put it in my pocket; however, knowing it was there brought me a comfort, almost the same way Brown Bear did. Almost.

That same year, my parents were diagnosed with cancer. I rummaged through drawers for that relic, convinced that it had something to do with my recovery, so obviously it would heal and cure them. It came with us to Mom's lumpectomy and radiation. I rubbed it all over my dad, like a shammie with carnauba wax on a new car, when he had his first surgery. Amidst so much unknown, I could count on the relic being in my pocket, no matter what. Until it wasn't.

It could have been hour 13 of 22 in the hospital while Pop struggled in post-op recovery. I reached for my relic and it wasn't there. We had walked around the building, taken different elevators and come in contact with at least 1000 people. Sheer panic consumed me. I convinced myself that if I lost the relic that people said brought me back from the dead, my punishment would be losing my parents. I couldn't control what was happening in my life, but I could at least keep a relic in my pocket, right?

It's messed up what I absorbed from others in matters of life, death, religion and obedience.

In the post-op waiting area, I sobbed uncontrollably, apologizing for not believing or being more respectful. A social worker sat with me while I cried hysterically.

I hope she was paid well that day.

The panic turned to acceptance. Here we were in a hospital surrounded by people going through the same trauma we were. Wasn't it possible that someone needed my relic more than me?

NO!

Then came the bargaining and the anger; no one needed the relic more than me. It was my relic! I deserved to have it! Ever the problem solver, Mom suggested I retrace my steps of the day.

After the nurses wheeled Pop into surgery, I had gone to the cafeteria to get breakfast for myself and Mom. That was 13 hours earlier.

Each step I took, I kept my eyes on the ground. I passed several custodians sweeping and emptying trash. This was a lost cause. Mom just sent me on my way because I was exhausting her.

I walked into the cafeteria to scout around the beverage coolers, hot bars and coffee station. Nothing.

All the tears had dehydrated me, so I grabbed a couple bottles of water and made my way to the checkout line, which happened to be the same one where I'd purchased breakfast. I lowered my head, completely defeated.

There she was, Mother Marianne staring up at me from my relic.

Man alive! I knew it! I am supposed to have the relic! My parents are going to live. I am going to be a better person!

Oh, yes. Here is your payment for my water, kind sir.

My relic and I have been through a lot. My relic played a role in my belief. My father did die, though years later. My mother has almost died a few times. My relationship with Mother is rock solid.

I have given the relic to someone else who needed it more.

I've arrived at the place where for me, it's no longer about the relic, but about the prayer.

Act III
Got Miracle?

"Don't ever underestimate the importance of
owning your own experiences.
People may define you,
but you have the choice to let them."

Survivor's Guilt

As the Miracle Girl, I'm frequently presented to people in crisis as the shiny package, the face of hope. I establish a relationship with these caregivers and patients. I invest emotionally and spiritually in our exchanges. It is a role I take on and view as one of the greatest privileges of my life. Sadly, many times when the patient dies, I become a reminder of a miracle that this group of friends and family won't receive. I accept this responsibility. I understand it because it all happens in raw, human moments.

I didn't know any of that at 17 when my aunt died of ovarian cancer, the disease I'd survived.

I wasn't yet officially in remission, and she was the first person in my family to die from the disease. As I stepped out of the car before going into the funeral home, my dad said to me, "This will be hard. A lot of people will be upset that you're here."

Here? Where is here? Here at the funeral home? Here on Earth?

I didn't know what to do with my body. I loved my aunt deeply.

We had only lived in Syracuse a year or so when she got sick; when she'd been well, I was sick, so our time together was mostly visits over gift baskets and scheduled around our naps and medications. Her husband, my dad's brother, was my godfather. We were close.

I was devastated by her death, but somehow I interpreted my father's warning to mean that I wasn't allowed to be sad.

No one said to me, "Don't be sad," or "You didn't know her well enough to grieve."

Instead, they said, "We didn't get our miracle," or "At least you got your miracle."

"She didn't get her miracle."

Two years before my aunt's death, I woke up from a coma, unable to move, walk, talk or function independently, and had no memory of the recovery, which apparently couldn't be medically explained.

People latched on with vice grips to the idea of me as Miracle; no one sprung for the colorful coat, but ironically, there was a complete disconnect to the challenges I experienced. In the process as a person, a mere mortal, the set of human emotions and circumstances were seemingly ignored.

I refused the miracle—not publicly, because I only knew about 15 people in town—but to my parents and in my mind. I believed it was the doctors and nurses who saved me. In my mind, that was pretty cut and dry.

There wasn't room on my plate for the entrapment of Miracle.

As people gathered around the casket toward the end of my aunt's wake, I felt suffocated. My face burned. I wove through the labyrinth of mourners and escaped into the ladies' room.

My breathing, now like a hunted animal, was labored and low. I stared in the mirror, grasped the countertop of the vanity, heaved... and sobbed.

The glow of the sconces and giant cabbage flower wallpaper blurred. Much of my respiratory system had been traumatized by my illness, and my intubation left me with significant scarring. This meant that when my breathing became more stressed, I couldn't utilize breath for my voice.

My body writhed and the tears poured down my face, but there was no sound, just controlled chaos in my skin, painful silence and utter loneliness.

The door squeaked open. NO! Only the stalls had locks. I scrambled to hide, with no success. It was a standard, small, funeral home ladies room. Though the print of my skirt matched the wallpaper, no amount of me pressing myself into the wall would allow me to blend in.

Wrapped in the arms of my aunt's daughter as her back faced the mirror, I caught my eyes in the reflection. I looked like a badger who got the wrong end of a ground beehive.

"Pull it together!" the voice in my head shouted. "It's her mom that died, you jerk."

I would be penalized for my sorrow, shamed for not focusing on my guilt and gratitude.

"People were wondering where you were," she said gently, softly.

Oh, my God.

Now, I'm the bloated, bee-stung, should-be-dead, glad-she-didn't-die, why-is-she-here, well-if-she's-here, why-is-she-in-the-bathroom, is-something-wrong-with-her, no-she's-a-miracle girl.

The next morning, I read a beautiful Irish prayer at the funeral, and I almost fell off the altar on my way back to the pew. My whole body was like gelatin. Every cell of my miraculous yet grief-stricken body shook and wavered.

Back at the house, I hovered near the food table, my refuge for fuel after the radical, self-chastisement experiment. Not that there weren't other lovely stations around my aunt and uncle's home featuring little bites or bowls of nuts and such, but this table was in the den, in front of the bay window, with less noise.

I stood close to the drapes, wishing they would envelop me.

Again, strangers and family alike approached me, saying things like, "What an incredible thing that happened to you..." or "We prayed for your aunt but...I guess it wasn't in the cards."

My hands became like the shovels on backhoes; the more people posited their disbelief to me, the greater the quantity I shoved in my face so I wouldn't have to reply. It is rude for a young lady to speak with her mouth full, though I'm not sure it's a prize to approach the light fare of a funeral like a pie-eating contest, either.

"You know..." the steady voice said to me as I stood to face the drapes. I swallowed hard; it was some combination of frosting and mixed nuts.

"I'm glad you're here." I raised my head to meet my aunt's son's face.

"Bhweally?" What can only be described as snack mist left my mouth with the question.

"Yeah!"

There was a lilt in his voice.

I needed a low-level, noninvasive Heimlich-type procedure to move the bolus through my esophagus, and yet at that moment, he saved me, validated me, comforted me, welcomed me, honored me and relieved me of my guilt.

It was guilt that wasn't explained to me, one I couldn't begin to wrap my head around and didn't know existed in me until just hours before the events of that day.

The Name's Miracle, Got Miracle

The catch phrase was born during a night out at a bar with a bunch of my closest frat brother friends, some of whom I on occasion made out with. As they came to know my story, they would joke that they "Got Miracle."

Remember, in high school I had one eyebrow, a goatee, leg braces and a swollen glow from steroids. I felt about as feminine as a red wood. No offense to the red wood and not to knock it for anyone else, but I was more than a late bloomer in college, and I was all for any chance to merge my miracle with seeming normalcy.

I took college head on: stats for the men's lacrosse team; member of the black student union; sexual assault response team; riverside players; young democrats. I signed up for everything. Well, freshmen year someone signed up for me; I still couldn't hold a pen because of the neuropathy in my hands. Like I said, I was a hot ticket.

Months prior to this night out with the boys, I had run for student government president. The decision was somewhat last minute and my campaign was based on slogans and ads my friends and I stole from magazine articles, celebrity gossip and current events. I cared very much about the issues, yet I didn't take myself seriously, what with my markers, glitter pens and glue sticks. I was raised on the old school charm of handshaking and chicken dinners for wannabe office holders. This was my grassroots take on things.

A gaggle of guys from one of the fraternities had their pledges pass out flyers all over campus, without my knowledge. I started seeing photocopied images of myself on lampposts and then duct taped on backpacks of students I didn't know. The guys used the slogan "Got Mahoney?"

Nothing about my run for this office was negative or rooted in counter attacks. I was gonna give it a shot and see what happened. I believed in the job and myself, and saw no reason why it couldn't be fun. The prospect of taking that approach into meetings, creating legislation and working with students, faculty and administration was exciting. People responded to that. I think they still do.

I called Pop to share my next generation marketing plan.

"Can you win?" he asked in a very intense and low tone.

Of course he would treat my college run like that of a high stakes federal campaign. I was crestfallen because I wanted him to respond to my excitement, not take me out of a game simply because I might not meet his expectation of success.

"Could you put Mom on the phone, please?" I was pissed, but asked like a lady.

I vented to her about my father's expectations of perfectionism and told her all about my posters.

Like the bridge builder she's always been, I heard her through the hand she placed over the receiver: "John. She's used glitter. It's all very festive." God love her.

I won the election and went on to help eradicate debt, protest lack of arts funding and have a couple verbal knock-down dragouts with different department heads over a variety of issues. The president of the college even had my parents and I over for breakfast. Pop told everyone I won by a landslide and that I was held in high regard at the institution.

Maybe I was. It didn't really matter. I was thrilled to be a version of myself that felt happy and honest. This was the side of me that I didn't let shine during the cancer years. I think that's what college was for me overall, a chance to wake up the parts of myself I let lay dormant during my illness.

My public and private life in college was all-encompassing. I had less fear about speaking my mind because I was Mahoney, I was Kate; I was not the Miracle Girl. I started school as a new kid at this place just like everyone else. We all had a past, we all had the autonomy to reveal our thoughts, dreams and histories as we chose. I entertained the possibility that it was safe to share again.

Doctor Professor Jason, we called him, was teaching a course on theatre and performance. My assignment was to deliver a piece I'd written about myself. I crafted a monologue about my cancer and how I was dealing with life or death… and how that was more important than prom or homecoming.

I stood in front of my classmates, in the green room of the theatre building. I took a deep breath—as deep as I could take since my scarred lung tissue still presented challenges—and began to tell my tale.

I'm not sure I made it more than three sentences in when the walls around me closed in, my voice started to shake and the tears came out like water from a burst pipe. I ran to the bathroom and locked myself in a stall. A couple of girls from my class came to comfort me.

I wasn't crying because my story was so sad, I was crying because I hadn't been truthful. The fact was my words were saying that I was wise beyond my years, beat death, didn't have time for frivolity in the face of cancer. The truth was that all I wanted was to blend in back in high school.

Faced with the reality that all that was being asked of me in this space was that I be myself, well, it was very overwhelming; up to this point, I was so used to no one really wanting to know any more than I thought they deserved to.

I pulled it together and returned to my place at the front of the class. When I finished reading, most people in the room had tear-stained faces, including Jason, who suggested I write a one-woman show that could serve as my senior thesis project.

We started with me on stage and him in the front row of the audience.

"Can you hear me?" I begged.

I didn't know if my voice would sustain or if I could even be heard in the back of the house in the theatre. I had a vocal surgery after freshman year. I worked with a voice coach, sang in the shower. I was determined to use my body and voice as my instrument.

Jason was like my life coach when we talked about me not being mic'd for the show. Once, halfway back in the house his yes's became no's. I cut out dairy and caffeine and tried to rest my voice whenever possible. I did breathing exercises.

About a week before rehearsals started, we returned the theatre.

"CAN YOU HEAR ME?"

I don't honestly remember his response or my reaction. I remember the feeling of complete fulfillment. That little girl in high school who couldn't be heard in a crowd of more than two because of her vocal trauma and organ failure just reached the back of the house with her voice. Another part of me came back to life.

Typically, each student had one advisor for the thesis process. I requested all three in the department because I wanted a more collaborative process, plus I felt I might learn more since each of these professors brought with them a different world perspective.

Dale was the dream big guy who was willing to support just about anything I proposed. He had a working knowledge of Kabuki theatre; he was just loving and Zen and had a crazy solid mind-body approach to his art.

Jason, though the initial cheerleader on this project, delivered frequent blunt force trauma with his truths. He schooled us on musical theatre and set design; everything needed a clean and clear reason to exist, but could also benefit from a peppy melody.

Thirdly, not lastly, I had another mentor in TM. He told me that no one wanted to see a show in which someone talked about themselves for an hour. This baffled and devastated me. How would I share my truths? Wasn't it obvious how powerful and unique they were?

That he could not answer, which only left me further perplexed.

I turned to the crew. One of my brilliant writer friends took my script and broke it into six monologues: three to be delivered by me as different versions of myself at ages 10,14 and 21; then three as me playing other characters: Mom, Pop and my best guy friend in Ireland. I would be Kate playing someone else pretending to be Kate, all while being Kate. Say that three times fast.

One evening after rehearsal, I called home to check in. Pop found a section of a script draft on his computer in which I addressed his drinking and rehab. I intended to be transparent in my art. I had not considered asking his permission because if anything, the catharsis of this show was also my chrysalis.

He refused to take my calls and shut me out of his life for almost two months. He said he and Mom wouldn't come to the show because I would have to play to two audiences, them and everyone else.

The next day, the crew and I tackled my monologue about that night Pop hit me in a drunken rage.

I called up to the booth to my lighting designer and friend, "Do you have anything that will make me look less puffy?"

In an instant, the stage went dark. He hit the blackout button. That was friendship.

The experience of creating and critiquing was as exhausting as it was exhilarating. We worked tirelessly up to opening night. I came to the theatre about an hour before curtain, convinced I didn't know any of my lines.

On stage, I remember performing lines from the script. All the while, another monologue played in my head: "No one likes what or who they're seeing."

The lights came up after the last line. My entire fraternity family was there, clapping and whistling, along with classmates and dorm mates.

I walked offset. TM was standing there. I somewhat sheepishly asked him, "Did I do it right?" He beamed and embraced me. I entered the hallway toward the dressing room. Dale stood at the door. I crumbled into his arms and sobbed. Jason came up behind me and wrapped his arms around me. It was all very dramatic.

The review written stated that my show was about my survival at the hands of an abusive alcoholic. There were 6 monologs in a 75-minute performance. Two sentences dealt with an isolated incedent of abuse. I guess that was easier for the reviewer to relate to than a childhood spent in chemotherapy.

My parents were right not to have come. We each deserved our own time to heal from what we'd separately and collectively endured. Besides, I basically had three dads with whom I worked around the clock. Still, I was utterly broken. I cried in every rehearsal and needed to take more breaks.

Before spring break, I learned that I had been awarded not only departmental honors, but also thesis honors for my show.

As I crossed the stage at graduation, I saw and heard my parents join in the cheers.

When a production is mounted, actors, dancers, lighting and sound designers, directors, dramaturgs, costumers, prop masters, stage managers, set designers, builders and playwrights come together with the intention of storytelling and a family forms.

My college family showed up for me and became a part of my story every day in some capacity during the four years we were students together and repeatedly for all the page-turning moments since.

They keep me grounded. They empower me. They are my people.

I've certainly Got Miracle.

Hang 'Em High And Holy Rollers

"You have abandoned your faith!"

A response on hearing I'd accepted a role in a stage play, which focused on women's minds, spirits, and bodies. Every time I play a role in which I am not a devout or virginal lily, someone somewhere questions my value system because of who I am in their mind.

"Your father is dying. He was a Liberal, and you should know his life was rooted in nothing more than selfishness and greed. He is going to burn in hell."

What can I say? You'd be hard-pressed to find that in a sympathy card. The balls it took for this person to speak their truth impressed me.

Most people want to connect with the human condition, putting the opportunity of the relationship first. I'm telling you that when I didn't tow the line, there were people—even in my family—who have taken ownership of me with their belief of who I'm supposed to be, to say, to feel, to think, to do. Because of what defined me in the eyes of these people, I've been verbally assaulted with unapologetic frankness and some not-so-Christian views.

It's true: I am a living, breathing vehicle of a documented miracle in the Roman Catholic Church. So yeah, in certain circles, I am a big deal. In my position as Miracle Girl, I've been wounded, scarred and horrified by some traditional evangelical folks who put me on a pedestal with pomp and circumstance, and simultaneously tear down countless others in the name of the same God they celebrate for my miracle. I have been bullied and victimized in my faith.

I was 14 when Miracle got slapped on me like a ketchup label. I've grown into my ideologies, just like every other young person in the world. My life has been informed by each and every experience I've had until right now. There are things I agree with—like respecting all people—and things I can't get on board with—like the exclusivity or lack of access to anyone seeking civil rights and equality. There I go again, speaking out of turn and pushing boundaries. So un-miracle-like.

"Touch me so I can be healed."

I don't remember where I was for this one, but it's when I realized I should probably be charging for events. One of our friends, a wonderful nun I've known since I was a baby, joked that I should be selling scraps of my old clothes.

"Will you talk to my friend and make him go to church?"

I will talk to anyone and hear them out. Be careful what you ask for, though, because I'm not in sales. I'm not in the business of pushing your agenda. If your friend isn't going to church, why don't you talk to him? Or skip church to be with him and see how that feels?

We have to meet each other where we are to get to where we want to be.

I genuinely don't want to give Catholics—or anyone—a bad rap. For every encounter that's offended my sensibilities, there are others that reaffirm the joy of my childhood faith, the comfort that my Catholic traditions have brought me in my life. This is my story.

I'm tired of hearing people say, "I would never... " or "I wish I'd known..." or "How dare you..."

Choosing church or any other bordered haven at the expense of relationship is not okay with me. Moral superiority grosses me out. Seriously, stop it. This can't be the first time you hear that hate blocks love or that fear is the opposite of love. If you want to know something, ask. And to those of you hiding, judging from the other side of your argument: just because people are yelling doesn't mean they have it all figured out. You're not alone. No one can micromanage your prayer life. It's yours.

We always have a choice. It's not easy. It's not pretty. It's not clear. But it will be yours to own. Sometimes I think people feel safer being mad than somewhat blindly walking into the fire and trusting that they'll get out unscathed.

If you want to say that your Catholicism is why you won't get divorced or talk to the homosexuals or listen to a woman who's had an abortion or vote for whatever legislation the media claims will ruin your life, that's OK. But examine your faith, your prayer life, your relationship with church and community, and your history in the context of your religion, and then tell me what your beliefs are.

I'm not going to live a life running toward a heaven, or away from a hell, so fast that I miss out on this mortal life I have here on earth, one for which I am profoundly grateful.

I am aware that not everyone wants the burden of taking responsibility for their feelings. They prefer to heed someone else's decree. It's not right or wrong; it's where they are.

In every life—relationship, religion or belief system—there are regrets. There is harm. I've learned that disease and crisis don't allow us to process emotions and information at a current pace and, by extension, we can only succeed retrospectively. And even then, no matter what, society rarely accepts an individualized pace for recovery from whatever ailment or circumstance of humanity it may be. We all screw up our lives and each other's lives at some point, and though we do have the chance to have it all, I don't believe we get to have it all—at least not all at once. There is comedy and tragedy in the normalcy of life, even when every day and sometimes every hour has a new normal.

This might feel like a lot. What I'm saying is that we often have a belief system different from our neighbors or friends. At the same time, we are all human and have infinite points of connection.

Humanity and divinity deserve equal respect.

Body Of Christ Dysmorphic Disorder

I was a few weeks post-op and had a followup visit with the gynecologist who removed my tumor. The table was motorized and covered in tissue paper. The ceiling lights were an industrial level of bright, and there was this spotlight on a stand—like a floor or reading lamp—unlike anything I'd seen in the theatre. I still didn't know exactly what a gynecologist meant for me. I was 14 and only had my period a couple times when this stage four, basketball-sized malignancy was removed.

I was wearing a hot pink tee shirt over a chartreuse tee shirt, and the sleeves were rolled up. I had on black boxer-type shorts with bright fruits and vines on them. It was a complete look from the a well known store circa summer of 1992, and one I was quite proud of. If memory serves, even my socks were doubled and then folded over to reveal an additional pop of color.

"Let your knees fall wide apart."

I heard nothing after that. Ultimately, the nurses had to hold my knees in place. My playful shorts were in the chair by the door, balled up with my pastel-colored day-of-the-week cotton underwear.

I could make out cabinet knobs, medical charts and the pattern of the floor tiles. There was an obligatory guest chair, my mom's hand in mine, and my hair on the paper pillow; it had started falling out in feather-weight clumps. No faces, no sound. There were hands, fingers, something cold and sharp—was it camping equipment?!

Every month, every three months, every six months, every year, the routine and this exam stifled a part my spirit with each visit. The clothing balled up would eventually be folded neatly in the chair, always on trend. My hair grew in and I needed no assistance mounting the table or assuming the position. To his credit, I was always Kate to my gynecologist, never the miracle girl, never a case study. He treated me with absolute professionalism and dignity. It hasn't always been that way.

One gynecologist called me out on not being sexually active enough. Another one dismissed my concerns in favor of asking a litany of questions about my time in ICU and the miracle. Then he asked if I knew that it was a healthier choice to eat a handful of almonds, as opposed to a sleeve of crackers.

With my feet in the stirrups, I was genuinely caught off guard. Like I wasn't already in a vulnerable position…what was going on down there that required any inquiry about snacking habits? It's safe to say that was new low.

At 14, I was too young to articulate violation. I was too young for all of it. The memory lived in me for years, followed me into relationships without my cognition. My whole identity as a woman had been framed by gynecological oncology.

When I was in my 20s, I still carried a belief that if I had sex, it would result in one of two things: cancer or pregnancy, both of which would further destroy my life. Mind you, I didn't think that for anyone else. I convinced myself that this particular logic-defying chain of events would be specific to me.

When I did decide to sleep with my boyfriend, it was less about being intimate with him and more about my being able to handle all my feelings of shame, guilt and fear. A very biblical, patriarchal weight followed me, hinting that my having sex would result in some sort of global catastrophe.

Because I pushed the miracle and the trauma away until I was out of my teens, my processing of it was also delayed. So how would you expect the Miracle Girl to react when she loses her virginity, and then turns on the news an hour or so later to see the World Trade Towers collapse?

I experienced all the same grief and devastation as everyone else, yet there was also this voice in my head that said, "Well. Sure. That's about right." Lucky for me, I got a call that day requesting that I come home to meet with a surgeon because my cancer labs were elevated. I couldn't make this up if I wanted to!

There were some doctors who felt if and when I was ready, I could potentially get pregnant, but my scarred body and history of organ trauma might not be able to tolerate or carry a pregnancy; that was another bit of knowledge that put me in conflict with myself. I had taken full ownership of a life plan that included only puppies, kittens and adoption if I could afford it, so I didn't care much that I might not host a baby.

I had this archaic messaging in my brain that told me if I couldn't deliver the goods, no man would want me. It all circled back to my hating my body for not being all things to all people.

It took me a long time to put words to feelings of inadequacy, anger, and resentment. I misread relationships and other dating scenarios. I found peace and quiet in eating disorders—starving, vomiting, binging—occasional binge drinking and routine negative self talk.

On the spectrum from Madonna to whore, I'm not sure where drunk barn animal fell, but I was definitely there as I navigated crushes, deeper feelings and the meaning of life as I knew it. Is it weird that in a way, bourbon and my gynecologist have been my longest relationships? Oh, and Jesus. Let's not forget him. So that's all mainstream and super relatable, right? Maybe not so much.

For years, I was elevated by others who wanted to have ownership of me, but not take the time to accept me. I've spent a lot of my life as Miracle Girl, feeling as though maybe I'm not meant to receive love, only give it and be sure every person knows they're worthy of it. And I don't mean worth in the sense of power play; I'm talking a love that is shared and accepted within yourself.

Obviously I do know love, and have love from the incredible, gracious, funny sages I have been fortunate to call parents, the friends who have saved me from myself over the years, and the occasional guy I let myself believe when he says he gets me. I'm still not totally sure I know who I am without fat jokes at my own expense though.

Love is the essence of every religion, right?

The order society tries to impose on it can sometimes cause more harm than good if we are to accept our body as our temple and celebrate it accordingly.

A Brief History In Pictures

Mom and Pop - my favorite love story

Pop and I lighting the advent wreath - one of our most sacred traditions

The Mahoneys move to Ireland

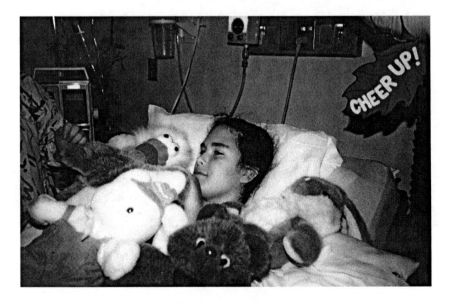

What I did on my summer vacation

Discharge Day

Act IV
Smoke and Miracles

"I have been knocked down, held back and thrown forward
so many times that I've almost lost count.
If it was more breathable, I would wear bubble wrap."

Vatican Vacation

I've been told that meeting the Pope is the earthly equivalent of being greeted by St. Peter at Heaven's gate. There are people who wait their whole lives to meet the Pope so they can die. That's a lot of eggs in one basket.

Between my days in the ICU and the big reveal of my identity in the local media some 20 years later, Sister Mary Laurence and I would touch base about my miracle case periodically. Each time, we would butt heads, because she was focused on the endgame: Mother Marianne Cope becoming Saint Marianne Cope. In this phase of my life, I didn't grasp that at all.

My life was about what I was doing on Friday night. I wasn't bound to an archaic institution, under the tutelage of a bunch of religious patriarchs in red shoes (part of the traditional attire—similar to the ones you can dye-to-match for the prom). A couple decades at the receiving end of well-intentioned evangelical messages labeling me as too much and not enough had temporarily soured my relationship with my church. My life was not yet about my connection to a possible Saint.

I continued to go to mass, but I didn't own this miracle. On the flip side, when asked questions, I didn't consider that my answers could carry the kind of weight that would ever in any way prevent a canonization, even if I didn't appreciate the magnitude of such an event. Maybe I wasn't invested in the ceremony, but I did love the nuns and I would never want them to be demoted or demeaned. They had become my family. I was questioning the actions of the man-made church teachings against the world I was experiencing, not my faith and certainly not the sisters.

In the beginning, I didn't possess the maturity or skill required to be diplomatic without coming off as dismissive; I couldn't be honest without risking divisiveness.

Once the word on the street got out that the Pope told the Bishop we would have a saint in Syracuse, my parents and I were invited to go to Rome to join in the celebration known in the Church as a Beatification. It is the elevation of a person, usually after they've died, in the running for sainthood based on a miracle attributed to them. There is a far more scholarly way of saying this; but this is a story, not a research paper.

After the Beatification was announced, but before our flight out of LaGuardia, my parents' dual diagnoses of cancer hit us like a tsunami. As Mom lay in bed in Syracuse, fatigued from radiation, Abby and I stood at Pop's hospital bedside in Manhattan, with splits of champagne to toast our upcoming trip to the Vatican, the "Church of churches." None of us knew if we would in fact all be well enough to make the trip.

Then the Pope died.

National attention was focused on the face of patriarchy, not the tireless, heart-filled work of the women, the nuns-my friends-and their fellow sister slated for posthumous promotion. I just couldn't let that go from where I stood.

The "empty seat" so to speak, did not stall our plans for celebration. White smoke would soon give way to Pope Benedict's leadership. Meeting the Mother Marianne Fan Club en mass would be his first big gig.

Next stop: the fabric shop for material to make mantillas!

A pilgrimage, if you don't know what that is, is similar to any other chamber of commerce-style organized trip overseas, except the stops along the way are usually chapels, statues or other edifices with religious and historical significance, not outlet malls. However, complimentary bags, hats, jackets and fanny packs were delivered to us in advance with our itineraries and name badges.

I know from the pictures that there were hundreds of people who left Syracuse and Central New York together. I see in the photos that I was seated in the terminal with many of the sisters, awaiting our departure. Unfortunately, I don't remember much about the stateside preparty because I was slightly distracted by concern for my parents and how they were managing the pace of everything. No one would have known that though when I turned around every now and again to yell, "COME ON!"

We landed at Leonardo DaVinci Airport. It was like a scene out of some screwball comedy; a sea of sisters, some in traditional habits, others in more casual attire seemed to take over the whole airport and spill into the streets.

We excitedly piled into coach buses, attended to by American and Italian Brothers, Friars and Fathers, and headed to our hotels.

Driving through the streets of Rome was like being in my elementary school history books. There was the site of Mussolini's hanging; the coliseum; the mount where Nero played the fiddle and watched the city burn. So cool, and only day one!

Mom and Pop, who struggled only a bit to keep up, looked adorable hand-in-hand, taking it all in.

There was little downtime within this pilgrimage to take on anything other than the aforementioned bus to tour the countryside. It was hard to know which way to go when each sculpture and fresco was more captivating than the next. Standing where St. Francis first worked with lepers was powerful; looking out the window where St. Clare prayed was inspiring. Every vista, every piece of art was mesmerizing. It was a cultural jackpot. Still, Abby and I had no problems squeezing in the more plebian activities of shopping, wine tasting, and photo ops at the famed Trevi fountain and the Spanish steps.

On the morning of the Beatification, my dear old friend Abby and I got dressed up and planned a day of sightseeing around the cobblestone streets of Rome. We were instructed to meet back at St. Peter's in Vatican City in time to settle in for the ceremony, before all the cameras started recording. There was worldwide coverage. It was a big deal.

We sat in Piazza Navona, sporting black dresses and big sunglasses, snacking on mozzarella, sipping on wine that was far more complex than the swill to which we'd both become accustom in college. We were our own movie. We were ladies lunching, just out and about, people watching and having a little lunch in Rome-simple pleasures in a grand adventure, all in a day's work.

Then the church bells rang out.

I knocked over the best batch of olive oil I'm destined to consume in my life. It spilled into my lap. Abby scurried to calculate and pay the bill—plus tip—and we took off like a shot, following the bells, hoping to get to the church on time.

Fun fact: the main door to St. Peter's Basilica weighs more than two young friends trying to open it.

We ran around to the side entrance, thinking we could casually slide in and take our seats. There was a small sign on the door, something about Papa. The door opened with ease. Abby and I darted in and made our entrance… onto the altar.

Yeah, that side door isn't like the side door of your local community center. It's definitely the Papal entrance.

Mom and Pop, you're welcome—for the olive oil, the messy hair, the tardiness, the giggling… all of it. I'm glad we could be here together. And oh yeah, the cameras were rolling. Neato.

We took our seats as my parents glared at us, and sunk in theirs.

What I remember about the rest of the mass is a blur. The newly elected Pope was not there; instead, I think every other member of the religious in North America and Europe was. Robes and hats, specific to rank and file, blended with flowers to color the aisles. Hawaiian customs were equally upheld on this sacred day. The collective sparkle from the sisters' eyes lit up the whole place. I still didn't really get it, but their joy was infectious.

After the mass, cliques of sisters and friends made reservations at trattorias and osterias around town. Somewhere between the Vatican and a dream, my parents and I shared one of the most magical evenings I've ever had in my life. Around me at the table were Abby, Mom, Pop, our friend Jigger, my ICU attending doctor, Russ, his wife Anne and their two kids, Robin and Daryl. The role Russ played in my case was pivotal. He penned the note stating my discharge couldn't be explained medically. He diligently worked to provide Sister Mary Laurence any documentation she needed along the way. They are super fun and silly and our families are totally in love with one another after having literally come through life and death and back again together.

A man of equal significance sat next to me: Dan, also my attending physician during my time in the ICU and subsequent stay in Progressive Care. He was less approachable in my hospital memory. Maybe it was the energy of the day, or maybe the wine that made me bring it up.

"You know, I was afraid of you," I delivered the reality with candor and caution.

"You?" he fired back. "I was afraid of you!"

Dan and Russ' kids were so little when I was sick, and my case was—well—it was intense, no pun intended. I hadn't considered what it must have been like to go to work helping a kid fight for her life, only to return home to tuck your kids in, hoping you never have to go through that on the other side of the stethoscope.

In an instant, our bonds renewed.

Dan and his kids, Laura, Emily and Matt, had flown all night to share in the festivities with all of us. Matt had just taken the SAT and slept facedown on the corner of the table.

These were people I felt truly knew me. Not that the pilgrimage or my time with the sisters on the whole wasn't powerful or joyful, because it was. I laughed until I cried almost every day we were on the road. This dinner was just a nice departure from feeling like I had to uphold the end of a bargain, instead of being a recipient of something for which I wasn't fully cognizant. Sister Mary Laurence and I were buds, but man, she was on a mission and I was not going to mess it up. On the journey to the ownership of miracle and self united, this night stands out for me as one of relief from no expectation.

The next day, I was back in the saddle for sainthood.

The Pope Story

Entering the Vatican auditorium two days after the Beatification mass, I joined 800 or more devotees of the newly beatified sister. I wore a sleeveless, geometric print dress that fell just above the knee and a pair of mules. Vatican-approved dress code it was not. Remember, the good dress was saturated with olive oil.

The Bishop of the Syracuse Diocese approached me and said, "You are going to meet the Pope."

I smiled, but was less than effusive with my response; due in part to the commotion, I was searching for my parents to make sure they were OK.

"That's why we're all here, right?"

He then explained to me that in fact I was going to present the Pope with the relic of our Blessed Marianne Cope. Setting the tone again, analogous to hooker with a heart of gold, I borrowed a jacket and a hairbrush, and compromised my posture so that my dress would appear longer. The Vatican isn't like a bowling alley; there aren't any extra shoes lying around. Honestly, when it comes to these public appearances, I always manage to look like I've just licked an electrical socket. Poise I can muster; polish, not so much.

I obediently took my seat in the front row, next to Sister Mary Laurence, who I knew had to be weary, but wasn't showing signs of anything other than elation slightly masked by more event-appropriate reverence. I continuously shifted, tugging at my dress to pull it over my knees. It was a futile effort.

The meeting of the Pope was the culmination of many people's life, work, hopes, dreams and faith. It bears repeating that this event was a big deal. It was also the homestretch of an epic excursion.

I turned to Sister: "Please don't take offense, but what are we doing after this? I am churched-out."

The fatigue appeared for a nano second in her eyes.

"Me, too," she acknowledged.

I caught a glimpse of the woman, not the steward. She was clearly genuinely ecstatic, dare I say giddy, yet a relief was apparent. Maybe she didn't know she was revealing that to me. Maybe she had been trying to tell me that all along. Maybe I was just ready to see it, here in the Vatican auditorium awaiting the Pope. This whole trip was one of awakenings and revelations, hitting home the reality that nuns are people too. I didn't realize I'd been labeling them the way I felt labeled.

Sister had a bargain to uphold as well. How had I not seen the full picture? We were in this together.

No sooner had I embraced this new working relationship with Sister and our vision, than I let my eyes drift around the great hall. On the altar, there were these sets and costume pieces that rivaled any scenic design I'd ever seen. Throne like chairs, gilded everything, more flowing robes with ornate stitching, more red satin shoes. And men. Only men.

The sisters, not exhibiting degradation in any way, dutifully sat in folding chairs on the floor in varying degrees of polyester fibers with cannonball size rosary beads. I wanted to scream out like the feminist and activist I was. An inhale of that proportion would have left me with a contact high from all the gold paint, no doubt.

The Bishop—who has never been anything other than lovely to me and always interested in my life beyond the miracle— returned to verbally secure the plan of my relic delivery to the Pope.

I offered, "What about Sister Mary Laurence? She may need help on the stairs."

With a gesture fit only for the patriarchy, he waved his hand.

"There are plenty of others to assist Sister," he said.

I kind of snapped.

"That may be!" I took a breath to diffuse my snarl. "But we're a team. We'll meet you on the top step."

I turned to Sister Mary Laurence and the sisters around me: "Stick with me, Sisters!"

The shattering of my glass ceiling was muffled by the sound of my father's voice cheering, "Viva Il Papa! Viva Il Papa!"

I am part feminist, part miracle, part humanist, part activist, part my great grandfather from Italy who would not condone my impulsive disregard for the Papacy and its sacred traditions. I sat, ankles crossed and to the side, hands folded silently, asking forgiveness. It seemed that every minute would be a milestone in self awareness and other directedness.

When prompted, Sister and I took our places at the base of the steps. We locked arms and began our ascent.

My actor brain turned on.

"Remember your blocking. Remember your lines," I told myself. Clearly, the costume notes had been ignored. Only a head held high and gracious words to match would suffice.

The Pope had kind eyes. He took my hands in his as he welcomed me.

"You are very blessed by Mother Marianne."

Wait for it...

"Yeah. Obviously."

Yep. That's what I said. To the Pope.

Strike two on the performance evaluation. To recover, I had to hit my mark when kneeling to kiss the ring-all part of the protocol when you meet the Pope, FYI.

We stood hands-in-hands for a bit. He told me I was the future of the Church, which was a lot to process. In my mind, jumping ahead, were thoughts like, "How I could come back from my brilliantly executed first impression?"

The Pope released his grip and swayed to the side. Harnessing laser-like focus, I went in for the kneel. I did not look up. I had a job to do!

Then it happened. CRACK!

I headbutted the Pope.

In an unprecedented move—everything, I guess, was unprecedented, given this audience was his first—His Holiness reached out to me for a hug. I missed the cue completely.

Did I gracefully shake myself off, reengage for the embrace? No. I did not.

I again darted up, as clearly was my pattern, and cried, "OH MY GOD! I'M SO SORRY!"

This was followed by my shrinking back down to an appropriate hem length, and whispering, "I'm so sorry I said 'Oh my God'."

In a flash, the Swiss Guard swept me off the altar, back down the steps to my seat next to Sister Mary Laurence, who resumed her disdain and resignation related to my apparent standard operating procedure. There were no words; just a look as if to say, "Really?"

So, maybe that's how not to meet the Pope, or anyone in a position of power with whom you think you may never have a chance in a lifetime to connect with again.

Regardless, I believe the message of the Holy Father to me is worth noting. He in his position represented the history of the church; I in mine, the future. We all have the capacity to be bridge builders. Maybe it doesn't have to end with a headbutt, it should always begin with a reach.

Exit Stage Left, Pursued By A Miracle

My first interview in Chicago was in conjunction with my audition for a drama program at a local grad school. It was 117 degrees. I looked at a map that only showed main streets, when in fact, there were over 24 streets between me and the theatre where I was interviewing. I wore heels. I arrived saturated. They offered me wet, cold paper towels.

The next interview required me to take the train. I rode all the way to the end of the line, only to realize I'd gone in the wrong direction and would now be very late. I arrived stressed. They offered me a drink and told me they'd gotten confused the first time they took the train, too.

This place was unlike New York. People were outwardly kind. Every big theatre seemed to have small theatres connected to it, like branches of a family tree. I didn't get into the graduate program, still I found a home in Chicago theatre. I moved once my mom was in remission and my father's tumors were stable.

To a person desiring stability, security, sanity, or some melding of the three, following your heart to the arts is fine, if it's a hobby. Hobbies are a wonderful escape from the rigor and demands of what nonactors refer to as "real life." To the untrained eye, an actor any less than celebrity isn't a success. I think there is some truth to that. My life, however, has proven it a misnomer.

I was an actor. My hobby was cancer. They were both a reality; the combination is a veritable definition of implausibility to someone who does not require creative expression as oxygen.

I'm going to sound like a snob, speaking as though all my debts have been paid by endeavors in the arts, like I have a status that enters rooms before I do. This is a lie; please indulge me.

In the arts industry, success is achieved though a blend of preparation, opportunity, funding, friends working with friends, timing, and yes—talent. All these things affect being cast in a production. If any one element is out of alignment, an actor (such as me) is frequently relegated to a job, or three, in some type of service. I've served tables, tended bar, seated guests, torn tickets, cleaned windows, vacuumed and scrubbed toilets. Service is a school in life that is home to working and out-of-work actors alike. There is never a shortage of characters, comedy or drama. That's the plus side of working for tips while changing the lights, waiting to see your name in them.

We are a band of outcasts, believing in magic and stepping out on faith. As our colleagues take on roles, join unions and headline on marquis, I'd be lying again to say that there isn't jealousy; but it isn't from missed opportunity, it's from opportunity yet to be seized. At least that's what we tell ourselves.

On my 30th birthday, I was in Chicago rehearsing a play. I was an understudy for a role that required me to work with a ventriloquist dummy. The character had social anxiety and used the doll to communicate. I found it challenging to have the conversations with myself even though every morning, for three years I stood in front of the mirror facing 18-hour-day seven-day-a-week jobs for no money to support my art. Each night, I switched the light on before entering my apartment to ensure the roaches fled back into the walls to meet the mice that ran alongside them. I developed a strategy using a bug repellant and large plastic cups that did the trick for any stragglers. Maybe I was more like my character than I could admit.

During rehearsal, the cast and crew brought cupcakes out on the stage and sang to me. I was euphoric! Casts and crews in Chicago got to know one another from different productions and various events, or through agents. This was my second big play at an award-winning space, with actors who held in their possession internationally-recognized awards. I worked as a house manager, bathroom attendant and bartender at this theatre, too. The fact that they took a moment out of their lives to celebrate me, for my life and as a cast mate, kind of took my breath away. In a flash, the candles and the house lights went out, and we were back in a scene.

Stepping out of the theatre that night was of equal celebration. A large movie company bought out parts of the building and the surrounding neighborhood, transforming it to look like the late '20s. They were shooting a sequence out front, so we were asked to wait until they were in between takes. I stood at the bar with my manager, quietly chatting about the day, and she offered me a chance to watch the filming from craft services. Two huge stars strolled by on their way to set, both in character.

I can't name them. We're not friends, yet.

Happy birthday, to me! I felt I couldn't open my eyes or ears wide enough to take it all in.

Yes, I was impressed by the celebrity. But to me, watching these professionals hit their marks and repeat lines and scenes with laser-like precision, was what it meant to be a working actor; it was going from job to job in your craft. Life hadn't afforded me the time to stay on my acting path long enough to be relied on that way. Every few months, I was in surgery or someone I loved was. I could only say no to auditions so many times before people stopped taking me seriously.

The director yelled, indicating the movie was wrapped, and the crews thundered in to tear down the set, my moment in history.

I'm quite sure my feet never hit the ground on my walk home. Even the roaches sensed a shift in my demeanor. The next morning, I had no trouble with my mirror pep talk. I told one of the regulars at the restaurant about my night.

She exclaimed, "Honey! I didn't know you were in show business!"

The thought of her excitement alone helped get me through more than a few auditions after that. The work I got was rarely soul-satisfying; it often gave me pause. My next director gave me notes nonplussed.

He told me, "If this were a movie, you would not be in it."

I'd chosen a career in which rejection was frequent, based upon what I could or couldn't be for a role. The miracle was not a part to play; it was part of who I was. Not being valued as myself was a burden I didn't always have the strength to carry on top of a career I was not able to sustain. The miracle gave me life. The illness vortex took life out of me. I wasn't ready to give in.

I had a couple understudy gigs under my belt, and word on the street was that one of the playwrights I had worked with was turning one of her plays into a movie. I wanted in. I left her messages several times a week, until one day, I got a call to come in for an audition. I read for the part of a granddaughter.

When I got home, the assistant director called to tell me that I wasn't right on screen for this. I was too old for the granddaughter, too young for the mother. She told me if I was interested in a non-speaking role she could send the script over. I said yes, please! After all, I was in the business of show! Why stop the momentum now?

I tore open the envelope to find my parts in the script, called sides. Were they sides if there weren't any lines? I read through the script, which revealed that my character was introduced in a flashback from the 1940s. Yes! I was the love interest for the main character, a woman. Well, that's new. In all my excitement, I never put together that this magnificent playwright who I'd come to call friend and mentor was not only a lesbian herself, but an award-winning lesbian playwright.

I was able to get a break in filming. It turns out that people who have one scene and no lines can do things like that and say, "I had a break in filming," which sounds far more extravagant that it truly is. Anyway, I had to fly back to Syracuse to drive my parents to Manhattan, because Pop's tumors had come back. I called the Mother House to request time together.

I sat at a round table in the solarium with three nuns closely associated with the cause for Mother's canonization. I shared with them that I was in a movie. They were excited. I shared that sometimes actors play characters different from themselves. I knew Mother would support my choice to give a voice to anyone voiceless, but I was legitimately concerned that in the wrong hands, my portraying someone whose lifestyle the church was so openly against could bring negative attention or harm to the Cause.

The sister to my right declared, "I like that you say you play characters."

The sister to my left offered, "I think as long as you don't do porn, it will be OK."

Aside from that being in the top five conversations I did not think I'd have in my lifetime, it was a positive reaction.

The sister across from me, Sister Mary Laurence, folded her arms, looked down her nose at me and posed, "Are you going to continue to play characters of seeming questionable morals?"

"Probably," I replied, with just a hint of defiance. Mary Laurence let her lips purse in way that told me she appreciated my asking permission, knowing I would have gone ahead with the movie even if she hadn't granted it.

Let me be clear: I didn't give a rat's ass that the church disagreed with the lifestyle of a woman I knew I would continue to respect and admire. Yes, it pissed me off; exclusivity always does. My primary concern was for the sisters and their plan for one of their own at the mercy of higher level Roman office.

Many actors stay in a wheel house that speaks to their upbringing and beliefs. I would never fault them for that. All stories need people to tell them. That said, I strive to try on characters like shoes, to know how I would walk in every one of them.

When Pop's cancer returned, I realized I might have to leave Chicago, never knowing the trajectory of a success I had only slightly tasted. I envisioned myself in auditions and interviews back east, where creative types would ask me what I'd done in this city of such immeasurable resources. Everywhere there was a "no" on my list, I made it a "yes." I missed the deadline for clown school. Yes, really. I was able to get into two improv courses, a field I only thought I knew.

The premise of improv is two words: "Yes" and "And."

If I say, for example, "I like your apple," and you say, "It's not an apple," you have closed the door on possibility. In turn, if I say, "I like your apple," and you say, "It's for the pie I'm going to make tomorrow," we have the makings of a scene.

Improv, like some of the theatre I studied in college, is based on creating something from nothing. There are practice games instead of formal rehearsal. The mind and the body are the instrument.

I found safety in scripted work, comfort in prose, and release in adlibbing; flying blind like this was wholly terrifying. Luckily, improvers live their lives in "Yes, and?"

When I said I was scared, they didn't say, "Don't be."

They said, "We'll show you. We'll help."

At the end of seven, weeks I got on stage, ready to lay my life down for my classmates. We ended up with a musical finale. I sang. I danced.

I think my final made-up verse was, "All I really wanted was a friend...Instead I got anarchy, and a fence." Maybe you had to be there.

"Show me, don't tell me," and, "Yes, and?" were drilled into us to shake out fear. Both forced us to utilize our whole selves for the sake of the work. It was exhilarating!

I remain indebted to those lunatics for helping me cross improv—a life lesson I didn't even know I needed—off my list, even if at the end of the day, I wasn't great at it.

I didn't want to believe that leaving Chicago could mean the dissolution of my career or that cancer and illness would yet again derail my dreams. There was a tugging in my chest, telling me maybe my kind of town was meant to be temporary.

Three full years passed before I "Yes, and-ed" my own life. My pride dragged behind me, like a tractor tire that had been run over by a combine spoke. I wasn't acting. I wasn't writing. I wasn't in school for either.

A call came from a youth leader at a church asking me to facilitate a retreat, meaning more than simply tell my story. I would be required to engage the students for a full afternoon. I pulled from my acting arsenal an exercise we used to create character.

I assigned the kids labels like cold or old, blind or lame and instructed them to walk around the room with only the label as their guide. They would do one lap around the space, and then we would discuss what they felt or experienced. One young woman scoffed that she was cold when she came in that morning, so she didn't feel any different under the guise of cold I'd put upon her. I paired her up with someone for the second time around.

When we gathered again, she reflected that she wasn't cold this time, but it was probably because she wasn't lonely and she didn't know she was lonely until she had a partner.

Now, if you are a teacher of anything, you know that this moment was pure gold to me.

The students engaged in a dialogue about the human condition through theatre. They were able to picture Mother Marianne not as a saint, someone inaccessible. They connected with her as a woman who wasn't a jerk, an attribute much more relatable.

I genuinely had no clue if my college acting class or my ability to share my course work would ever translate. When it did, something broke open in me, giving way to a part of myself I had been waiting to unleash back into the world. They absolutely wanted to hear more about my encounters with famous people, what it was like to work on movie sets and what show I would be in next.

I've been saying, "This is my show, for now," for over four years. I write, produce, collaborate, set props and handle contracts, in addition to engaging audiences of all sizes in venues nationwide.

I am an actor. One of my hobbies is still cancer. This is my reality.

I Didn't See The Iceberg

I was not ready to leave Chicago, nor did I want to. The Midwest, Lake Michigan, the live theatre of public transportation, all of it synonymous with home.

Mom had called me from the closet in the guest room, so Pop wouldn't hear, to tell me about her hip replacement. She burst into tears. She didn't want to ask me to come home. I didn't want her to ask me either. But there we were in all the emotions of the moment.

I told my supervisor at Children's Hospital that I would be heading back to Syracuse.

She smiled and said, "That's where your miracle occurred. Of course you are going back."

She was wise, whether I agreed with her on this point or not.

A slew of my magnificent comrades helped me pack up the moving truck, load by load, box by box. Toward the end, I stood to view what appeared to be 100 tote bags lining the hallway. Like souls in the bread lines of the Great Depression, these bags held my hopes and dreams and were about to be heaved into the unknown, not sure what of would befall them.

Really though, what kind of person had this many totes?! I should have seen the baggage as the omen it was.

I broke my lease, quit each of my three jobs, emptied my apartment, drove in the opposite direction of my career and personal goals, and returned to Syracuse, a place I'd been trying to escape since the moment I'd arrived.

"If your mother dies, I have no one!" He wept.

I knelt in front of Pop as he sat on the toilet, under the red heat lamp in the bathroom off my parents' bedroom. He was taken aback to see me, convinced my grand return was somehow related to Mom's prognosis. He was ill-prepared to have my mom go through something from which he couldn't save her. Granted, ever since doctors made the switch to modern anesthesia in place of a sharp stick and a bottle of moonshine, a hip replacement hasn't been directly linked to death since the 1700s, at least to my knowledge.

God bless him, in his sixth year with this disease-the primary liver cancer that should have killed him in less than two. Pop was vulnerable. In theory, it was a territory unfamiliar to him, though historically well-travelled. Publicly, he could still toss one-liners and strategize with ease and accuracy; privately, he was not able to maintain as high a standard. I didn't know then that I would be one half of a team, flanking him in strength in both worlds.

"So... I'm gonna go... wrap up," I sighed, further deflating myself. The body that hosted my wounded psyche headed back out to the driveway.

I pulled down the door of the truck and locked the hatch, quite literally closing a chapter of my life.

Truth be told, several other factors shoved me back to this apparent Mecca. The market crashed. The restaurant cut back shifts. Theatres weren't selling as many tickets for shows starring actors who still needed training. My rent was going up. And my medical bills weren't paying themselves. I had major surgery every year I was in Chicago. My tonsils, appendix and another chunk of my remaining ovary each had their swan song.

My scars are like fridge magnets: tokens from where I was and when, and what happened there.

Taking On Water

By December 8, 2009 we'd packed a year's worth of festivities into five weeks and Mom had her hip replacement as planned. We'd created a holiday calendar that followed no religious or commercial order: Thanksgiving came after the rest of America, Christmas two weeks before the birth of Christ and Mom's birthday thrown in a month ahead of schedule, because bubbly booze was not advisable on post-operative pain meds.

We'd started celebrating non-traditionally years prior, when the spirit moved us so as not to let illness snuff out our milestones. For this holiday season, we wanted to ensure we'd been happy and healthy-ish, together one last time, if that's what was meant to be.

Pop's care plan required hourly documented assessments, tracking medications, hydration, meals and rest. He experienced what in the liver world is called temporary hepatic encephalopathy; in his case, the organ could not process protein effectively, which resulted in elevated ammonia levels in fluid surrounding the brain. He exhibited a range of behaviors from aphasia-like reactions to physically violent outbursts, lacking ability to respond to basic cues and inability to identify familiar people, all with no memory of any of it.

It was a 24-hour job that ranged from praying he would make healthy choices on days he was well enough to go to work to detailed charting, verbally shared with the staff in the emergency room. No two days were the same.

It was most helpful for two people to operate on a system of tag teaming. My teammate was sidelined.

Pop was useless in Mom's absence, which was not otherworldly. She was in fact approximately three miles from the house, recovering in a rehab facility, not in the wilderness fending off packs of wild dogs alone. As he navigated his own illness and all the accompanying challenges, his ability to process and communicate feelings required emotional armor and patience. If he couldn't get to say, the Taj Mahal, how could he go to the corner store? In fairness, his compromised immune system, the side effects to his medications, the whole package of symptoms he was experiencing put visiting my mom in a care facility on par with licking handrails in a subway station.

To his credit, this was all tremendously demeaning for a man who started his career writing speeches that resulted in legislation benefitting the whole of the country. Conversely, if I wasn't so enraged by his inability to make his own lunch while I was communicating with doctors around the clock and constantly reprioritizing household chores, I would have found his grieving the distance from his love endearing.

Insult added to injury within all of this as he refused to voice his acceptance of my return home as the mandate it was. Every exchange with me was a reminder that I had no boyfriend, no job and no graduate degree. Each dagger was well-placed, yet followed almost immediately by a request for laundry, medication dosing, meal prep or other labors conveying task-based love.

My favorite was being on draft patrol. A mythical breeze followed only him wherever he went, requiring the coverage of anything from a small neck scarf to a wall tapestry to block it.

Five weeks was all the time I'd been home. I was still brushing my teeth before leaving the house, working out every morning and speaking in full sentences. I didn't know at the time that there was a chance I'd piqued.

I kept a voicemail from him asking where I hid his sandwich. I can laugh at it now because I appreciate how lost he was without my mom, shaken by all the unknowns, both with her prognosis and his own.

I learned that all the moving parts of assisting loved ones navigate and sustain chronic, terminal illness were what make up the life of a caregiver; always on the ceiling or the floor, rarely on level ground, living as the ball in a pinball machine, never sure when you'll be hit from the front, back or side, knowing only that when you are struck, you will fall temporarily in a hole. With any luck a pleasant tune will play.

The first time Pop had an episode, we thought he was having a stroke. It was terrifying to see this former orator and showman pantsless in a chair in the living room, unable to hold a cup, swallow water, find words or recognize his wife.

The last time it happened, he introduced my mom and me to his nurse as his brother and sister-in-law. Mom turned to me delighted and asked, "Who do you want to be?!"

That Mary Rose, she's my mom and will always be my favorite tune; that's why it was so scary when things in her recovery shifted dramatically.

She was discharged from the rehab facility on New Year's Eve day. We came in through the front door of the house so she could take in the Christmas decorations we'd left up in the living room. She was tired just from the trip home and ready to take a nap. I tucked her in bed next to Pop, who was resting, and jostled him slightly to let him know she was home, his bride he'd been so anxiously awaiting. When he turned over, we knew he was not alright.

He was in an ammonia spike. He had no idea who my mom was or where he was. He was quiet and comfortable, so I went about the business of getting someone to come and help Mom at the house. Then I called the doctor to tell them we were headed to the ED, packed a little bag for myself with snacks, water and toiletries, knowing all too well that that it would be a long night. He was admitted. I stayed through the morning. Happy New Year.

When I got home to take care of Mom, I found her in bed with terrible color. She was somewhat listless. She had contracted an infection while in rehab that apparently went untreated. I called Pop's doctor to request that he stay in the hospital a while longer; he couldn't come home with his risk factors until we knew what Mom had.

I called home care to take blood and assess Mom. They started her on an antibiotic. I cleared the guest room, no small task; it was filled with boxes, bins and linens from Easter of whatever year we ironed linens last. Pop could come home, but he and Mom had to be in separate beds and use separate bathrooms. Thank God I had training in hospitality.

Pop came home, not knowing Mom was there, since he had no memory of the last couple days. He couldn't hug her or get near her. So he stood at the doorway, crying happy tears. The two days that followed were more of the live theatre we'd come to embrace. My parents, on opposite sides of the house, called each other throughout the day from their cell phones and pretended they were on a cruise. They used nautical terms like starboard, portside and coming about. I was entrenched in laundry, meal prep and medication management. Clearly, I was steerage.

Still, I was happy to be on board with them until the next sea change.

Mom finished her antibiotics, but it turned out to be a strain of infection that didn't respond to that course of treatment. She weakened again, more rapidly. Pop hadn't been sleeping, eating or hydrating well. I called the nurse to request that someone come to the house to draw blood and assess Mom again, because I needed to take Pop back to the doctor for what I could tell was another ammonia spike.

The voice on the other end of the phone wondered why I wouldn't take Mom immediately to the hospital. I explained I couldn't leave my father incapacitated, as he could have been a danger to himself while in an episode with the encephalopathy, whereas a nurse could get labs so we would know Mom's levels and determine the best course of treatment. I got Pop in the car; the nurse arrived to stay with Mom while we went to the doctors.

The doctor examined Pop and drew his blood to get a sense of what his status was. A call came from the visiting nurse that Mom's potassium was bottoming out. She was at risk for heart failure. The doctor and I had a detailed conversation using only our eyes. I escorted Pop back to the car; she called an ambulance that would meet us at the house. I called my cousin to come and sit with Pop.

We pulled into the driveway just behind the ambulance. I gave Pop his meds and made him some food while the EMT's transferred Mom's totally limp body from the bed to the stretcher. My cousin arrived.

I held Pop's face, explained that I would be home soon and told him that even though it seemed really scary, the best place for him was at home, following his care plan, and the best place for Mom was at the hospital. One of the EMTs motioned to me that we were good to go.

I got in the car and followed them, lights flashing, unsure of whether or not Mom would be alive by the time we got to the hospital.

Once she was stable, Mom was admitted and stayed in isolation at the hospital for 10 days. It was the first time in her life that she'd ever had a room to herself. Pop held his own, but the stress—something he'd been told by doctors to avoid—affected his health visibly. I operated on adrenaline alone. Looking at a calendar, I was unable to pick out a night during which I'd gotten more than three hours of sleep. I was at the eight-week mark since my move back from Chicago. I had no idea that it was just the beginning.

Over the course of the next four years, Pop would have trips to the hospital on average every 11 days. He suffered five strokes and a broken hip. Mom recovered fully from her infection and hip replacement, only to be diagnosed with a tumor about a month before Pop died. The tumor was believed to be benign, however, it wrapped around the main blood supply in her brain, so there was risk for blindness, loss of leg function or death. If we were going to tackle something, why not make it a triple threat? It was successfully removed three short weeks after we buried Pop.

She lost her husband and her sense of smell during a season in which sense memory was at its most poignant.

I wasn't fully aware of all my losses, so just to stay on track, I periodically went to the doctor for mandated feel-good visits, where I would pay money I didn't have to be reminded that I was fat and tired. I received a diagnosis of exhaustion, a less festive way of saying I needed a long winter's nap. It did make me feel a bit like a celebrity.

The cruise line on which I envisioned myself headlining turned out to be a sinking ship.

Shipwrecked

Mom and Pop served as lighthouses, ports for the various storms in my life. With Pop gone and Mom recently recovered from brain surgery, I felt more lost at sea than ever before. In theory, we were on the other side of the trauma.

I found that while I was in a crisis, people could see that their words supported me. As the more visible, tangible crises blurred, or more aptly, their lives continued unchanged, people's approach differed. The mourners became the inquisitors. Through no fault of their own, it spoke to the human spirit that my loved ones wanted me to move on. Still, being asked what was next while I was processing what had just happened overwhelmed me.

I had written emails to people to keep them in the loop about my parents' cancer journeys. Behind the keyboard, I was able to edit my words and communicate a balance of funny and sad. I thought they were accurate. I looked back at some of my notes, unaware how many times I had expressed in words that we were okay, ready to move ahead. It may have been true in a fleeting way.

I was worlds away from anything resembling a life I wanted or believed I'd ever have again. I yearned for home, but had no idea where home was, even within my own body.

Less obvious scars are more like film developing; they appear over time, after being shaken to expose.

I had panic attacks that floored me and took my breath away. I had anxiety attacks that left me unable to hear or see. I had migraines that left me feeling as though my head was held in a vice, so the ice pick could strike intermittently with greater accuracy. The antidepressants gave me dry mouth; the sleep meds knocked me out, but didn't keep me asleep.

I became defensive, reactionary and short. To me, that meant only that I should have less interaction with people. Forget about sunset or sunrise; I stopped caring about life in my own body, let alone outside my house. No one needed to see the out-of-work actor or the Miracle Girl appearing ungrateful.

Each time I looked in the mirror, it was like seeing shadows. I literally saw and felt darkness everywhere. There were more than a few nights I went to bed with my fingers wrapped around a bottle of pills, making a list of all the reasons to take them, and another with all the reasons not to. I lived months in a cycle of closing my eyes to wait out the night one more time, only to open them to more of the same despair. Each step I took was one in quicksand with an anvil on my back.

Mom didn't like the word "suicide." What would people think?

People have strong opinions about suicide, the same as they do miracles.

I interpreted this, too, as another way I'd let her down. If I had taken my own life, all that I'd given my parents would be forgotten. I never felt I was sacrificing or losing out as long as I was caring for them, giving back to them, loving them. I didn't have one tangible thing to my name; my self worth and worth on paper were as blank as the resume I hadn't filled in the years I'd been home.

In death, I feared I would be more of a disappointment than in life, because this act would be viewed as something I did to her, not for her.

If I killed myself, I'd be the girl who killed herself. I was already the Miracle Girl. Neither title gave credence to the work in between. They were only labels that defined one moment instead of the whole story. No matter the direction, I constantly had guilt over not being able to be who she needed.

These feelings didn't all come on at once. Each part was present in varying degrees of manageability. Gently, that which I'd held deep inside—certain elements easily identifiable, others less so—made their way to the surface, until I was literally falling apart from the inside out.

I was diagnosed with PTSD. I had become a patient, again. The vicious cycle of trauma finally broke me. I enlisted allopathic and homeopathic practitioners. I fought harder than I'd ever fought for anything in my life, for my life.

In the mirror, I saw myself again—a person I thought I'd lost forever. I smiled back.

My Eleven O'Clock Number

My miracle doesn't make me less human: If anything, it makes me more human.

Being a survivor means even though I believe in something that is greater than myself, I've come to recognize that I am a part of that something, and the part I play is significant. It matters. I matter.

I'm still going to buy the tee shirts and support the causes. I'll light the candles, join the celebrations and wipe the tears. I'll continue to have moments when I walk into a room and feel I don't belong because to others my survival may appear to have come at the expense of another, or they might think my status is being used to disconnect rather than empower.

I will always hold in high regard the church communities who raised me. My story has never been about losing or gaining faith anyway. Mine is a story that humanizes faith, the divine comedy and tragedy.

Whether you worship a God that takes shape as trees or moon; whether your decisions are influenced by a holy book or other sacred text; whether you believe in science or coincidence over spirit; my role as a survivor is to always allow space in my mind and my heart for your beliefs.

My label of survivor means nothing if I wear it contextually and compete with anyone else on their journey.

My moniker of Miracle is nothing if I use it to separate myself from the rest of humanity and the circumstances within that. My job is to serve above all else as a reminder to you that you deserve and have the right to believe in yourself.

What you do, what you say, what you think, what you feel and what you believe matters. You matter. You have a voice.

Don't be a jerk, though. Pay it forward. If you matter, then let the person next to you know they matter. You don't have to agree with them.

How hard is it, really, to leave a small part of yourself open to the reality that everyone around you is surviving something? If per chance, it's nearly impossible, think of how it feels to know that someone else believes in you and supports whatever it is you are trying to survive.

Try to embrace equality and love as the root. Maybe you're still in the doubt and fear place. I get it. Well, I got miracle, actually. So, no worries; I'll believe enough for both of us, for all of us.

Act V
The Misfit Miracle Girl

"Survivor to me means not having the need to know.
It's about welcoming what's in front of me
regardless of what it may seem.
Life doesn't have to make sense for me to live it."

Re: Mission

Somewhere between having the seams in my pants let out and a decision to live a life devoted to self-loathing, my phone starting ringing with requests for me to speak about my Miracle. Pop was dying, Mom was recovering; why wouldn't I want to get up in front of a crowd?

At first, I was paid mostly in cookies, sparkling punch and feelings. This was fine because I was so used to being pimped out for this miracle that it didn't occur to me I already possessed the tools and passion for advocacy that could solidify an actual career.

Each time I told my story, a different person would approach me afterward to tell me a story. Often it would be something they had never told another soul. (Relax, I'm not hiding any bodies.) Usually, it was about a faith journey of some kind, an illness or loss of a loved one; something they felt only I would understand.

Quietly, my path was clearing.

Once I started asking for money, I hit another road block. Many people felt that to share my story was my mission. They weren't wrong, but it was hard to drive places, carve out time and prepare my speeches—and I did always try to do my homework to create a more personal engagement with audiences—with no income.

There were those who questioned my character based on what they felt they knew of my family's progressive politics or the roles they had not seen, but heard, I'd acted. They boycotted events, but called to express their horror at my life choices. This was particularly entertaining to me, as I'd quit my three jobs, all in various levels of a service industry, to move home and care for sick and dying parents. Last time I'd checked, that was straight-up Jesus' style.

Eventually, audiences began to understand that I was more than the story they had concocted in their minds. It had everything to do with me embracing it, too. I unintentionally fell into joy speaking and writing about this event in my life. However, it wasn't paying the bills.

I will share two job interviews with you. Each happened after my dad died and after my mom had her brain tumor. The first was for a job at a grocery chain, where no one knew anything about me; the second, at a big firm where I'd been invited for the express purpose of being a miracle.

I dressed nicely, brushed my teeth and wore a bra—all pluses, given what I'd been able to manage only months earlier. I filled out my application on the clipboard and took my seat in front of two managers.

Q: "Please share with us the best experience you ever had with a boss."

A: "Sure! After I graduated college and quit my first job, my boss was really supportive. I've never forgotten that."

Did I mention being president of student government in college? Did I mention being promoted in two different jobs each year for three years? I did not. I've had and kept multiple jobs, which have resulted in lifelong friendships with former bosses, the one I referenced included. Did I share that fun fact? I did not.

Q: "Please describe an average week in your life."

A: "Sometimes I read. Sometimes I watch TV. Sometimes I go out. Sometimes I stay in." It went on even longer...

WHAT WAS HAPPENING? I'd completely lost the ability to speak, to connect with or impress anyone in the human race. Plus, I failed to reference that I had just come off a job that kept me awake and tending to matters of life and death for no less than three solid years, without a single shift change.

A call came a few days later telling me they were going to go in another direction—for the job bagging groceries.

I sent up flares to friends, family and fellow parishioners. I tried to find jobs that were more traditional to make a living. A potential speaking gig had promise.

I walked into the corner office, of which two walls were windows looking out to a great, big, wonderful world. I was greeted by three older white gentlemen in well-tailored suits. I had been told they were looking at me to fill a gap in the religion sect of their company; this was a meeting in which they would "kick the tires." Desperate for work, I didn't stop to interpret that phrasing to mean I might be too young or too female.

I, as myself—casual, non-polished, believing we were just getting to know one another—pitched my miracle as though I was already enough. Far exceeding a suggested elevator pitch, I wrapped up, looked to the head of the group and waited openly for a response.

"We don't do that."

I was at a loss. I tried to ask questions; they countered with directives I think they believed were being given with wisdom and support. The truth was we were not the right fit. I should have just gone to the break room and talked with strangers. I would have made a more lasting impression. At one point, they told me a story about a man who had lived through an avalanche and how they were inspired. I couldn't disagree; it was a tremendous thing. It wasn't what happened to me, nor could I speak to it. Was that a polite way of telling me to throw myself off a mountain?

They then began a conversation about something else entirely, and proceeded to talk over and around me. I had been dismissed before—passive aggressively, too—but not in a meeting for which I was the invited talent.

I stood and excused myself. I shook hands that held little grip, and left with a sense that had I stayed, perhaps I might have been asked to take their lunch order.

I made it out of the building and around the corner before bursting into tears.

It took a good six months for me to shake that interview off entirely. My pain gave me purpose. I dove back in; booked talks for large and small audiences, facilitated retreats with students, shared dialogue in smaller more intimate groups.

With each passing day, my gut got stronger, my skin a little thicker.

The hardest part hasn't been people I know and love saying things like, "I'm just really sorry your life hasn't worked out." Each time though, it was as awesome as it sounds. In my attempt to communicate process to people for whom things only make sense as product, I convinced myself they were right.

People either do believe in God or they don't. They do believe in miracles or they don't. They do believe in themselves and each other or they don't. It isn't my job to make you believe. I can only tell you that I do. What is of consequence is whether or not you respect my beliefs.

We have to meet ourselves and each other where we are, with compassion at all costs. This doesn't mean we won't disagree or disconnect. It goes much deeper than that; each person and their place on this earth is one to be honored, dignified and supported as the embodiment of opportunity, deserving of gratitude. It is not a matter of right or wrong, good or bad; rather it is a knowing that sometimes we will challenge, refute or judge everything while simultaneously, somewhere deep inside, where the words don't come as quickly, accept that we are one.

Humanity is a tricky business.

People believe almost casually, impulsively based on circumstance. Miracle is perhaps not used as candidly, but it too has become something that denotes exclusivity. I argue that when pressed for reasons, why we do or don't believe in something boils down to owning the reality that we are no better or worse than the person standing next to us. That can be terrifying.

How do we know where we place in life if, at times, we can't justify where we can or can't see ourselves?

What is it that we will or won't do that establishes us in our convictions?

Between the mirrors and hurdles we set up, it's a miracle we aren't all hospitalized for injuries sustained while in competition and comparison with ourselves.

The truth is no matter what box we put ourselves in or others pigeonhole us into, each life lived is frequently one defined by isolated incidents, perceptions and misperceptions of others. If you need to scream out that you are or are not what people say you are, figure out why putting yourself in that kind of fight is so important to you. If you say you don't care what anyone thinks or says about you, look inside and find out what makes you someone who believes you need only yourself to rely on.

We all have a mission. Parts of us know what it is; they just have to wait for the other parts to catch up.

My Body Politic

I took a class on women in film back in college. We met once a week to dissect the roles portrayed on screen and in scripts. Part of our final grade involved comparing and contrasting two films, and two characters.

I chose two well-known films in which the same actress starred. In one, she was a recovering alcoholic charged with protecting a child, the irony of which was that her own children had been taken away from her because of her addiction and subsequent negligence. The other role the actress took on was that of a nun who chose to give dignity to a man on death row.

In each of these scripts, my group found that these women were written in a way that they were defined by society and judged by other women harshly as frequently as they let society dictate their place. We did a side-by-side comparison with two of those giant TVs and VCRs on rolling stands. Both characters were believed to not have maternal instincts or the capacity to mother, based on career or other pitfalls in life.

I remember being really upset that the writer didn't give the women power or choice over their circumstance. I suppose it was the time; though the only difference in the gender pay gap, or any other gap for women between then and now, is due to either more or less dialogue and attention.

I don't often recall my experience in that class. In fact, I hadn't thought about it since graduation. Then I had a hysterectomy, and it was like I was right there again, only I was fighting for and against myself.

My diagnosis of germ cell ovarian cancer came only a month or so after my first period. My first pelvic exam, pap smear and major surgery came shortly after that. In the years that followed my cancer, I had four cancer scares, three cystectomies, one polypectomy, one inoperable cyst, two DNCs, two adhesion removal surgeries, adverse reactions to three different types of birth control designed to quell cyst production, a diagnosis of PMDD, head aches, nausea and depression that shadowed my cycle like the angel of death, and challenges with weight gain. During an emergency appendectomy, doctors unfamiliar with my case wanted to cover their bases, so I was given six pelvic exams by six different doctors.

No one ever asked me how I felt about all these complications with my reproductive system. And I thought no one else was talking about their periods running their life, so it must just be the way it's supposed to be. I would continue to take it for the team, so to speak, well into my adulthood.

Eventually, I ended up bleeding so heavily I had to hang on to the wall to get to a phone and call my doctor. I called Dr. Mark's office. I mean, let's face it, he did my first surgery and my first exam. We have this weird bond that transcends gynecology because of how young we both were when we met as patient and doctor in crisis for the first time. Does that still technically make him my boyfriend?

Maybe.

Kidding.

His nurse told me to get to the emergency room as fast and safely as I could. Not convinced I was in danger, I told her I didn't want to bother the staff and could happily wait until an office appointment became available. She responded that the staffing shouldn't be a deciding factor, as she was more concerned that I might bleed out and die.

So much drama.

I arrived at the ER with my mom. One of my nun friends met us there. I was put in a wheelchair because I was losing conciousness. All my vitals were taken and I was led to a procedure room where a tech administered a trans-vaginal ultrasound. Always nice to meet new people. And that was probably all the sex I was going to have in another batch of calendar years.

Surprisingly, my bloodwork showed that I was not anemic. The ultrasound revealed a remarkable ovarian cyst. I was thrilled. Any opportunity not to waste hospital resources and prove myself right was a win. My psyche was fragile in the context of my own woman's health. The attending sent me home and I scheduled a consult with Dr. Mark's office to discuss my options.

His PA was able to see me right away. I bellied up to the table and stirrups like a regular at a dive bar. She walked in with a filing box, explaining that she hadn't had a chance to catch up on my case. I gave her the abridged version, one that would fit on a sticky note as opposed to a flash drive. I brought my list of questions and concerns, and we engaged in thoughtful dialogue.

I didn't think she was repetitive, but I felt like I'd heard her mention my young age as a reason not to do a hysterectomy more than a few times. I could feel my face getting hot, my chest and throat tightening. I'd considered a hysterectomy before and after several different procedures, but had always deferred to the practitioners or even my mom. I went to war in my own body and mind, because after everything I'd survived, I didn't believe I deserved to make the choice.

I finally said, "If this is about having a baby, I don't need to be able to birth a child to be a mother."

I might have said it with a bit of an exasperated tone. There was silence.

I continued, "From where I sit, I'm done."

She didn't try to scold or sway. She was instantly supportive and responsive. She scheduled me for surgery with Dr. Mark days later. I immediately went to work researching hysterectomy challenges, complications and called on the women in my life for advice. I was blown away by the knee jerk negative reactions to my inquiry.

"Are you sure it's really that bad?"

"So you just don't want to be a mother?"

"What does your mother have to say about this?"

"Is it cancer?"

"Is your mom upset because now she won't be a grandmother?"

"What if you meet a guy and he wants to have kids?"

I was stunned by womens' inability to meet me where I was. Instead, they projected their beliefs, judgments and fears on me.

There was balance though, almost in equal ratio.

"Your vagina does not define you!"

"It is 2016, you have the right to make this decision."

"You are more of a mother to our friends' kids than some of the mothers I know."

"Having this surgery was the best decision I ever made."

"Celebrate you, Kate!"

I reached a place during the preparation for my surgery and recovery in which I needed to be completely alone. The noise of everyone weighing in—pro or con—was an unsettling distraction which evoked doubts in me. Again, what if no man would love me? Who am I without my self-deprecating fat jokes? Why is my pattern to look to others to affirm choices that aren't theirs to make? What if I grow a beard, cry all the time and start craving cat food? I don't know any guys who want to date that chick.

I actually posed that question to Dr. Mark in the operating room before surgery. He laughed and rolled his eyes.

Then he said in his signature matter-of-fact tone, "I don't think anything has been working for quite some time...once we remove the problem, I think you're going to feel a lot better."

Just hearing him say that—knowing I was in his hands, and he had participated in, and not just witnessed my history—all my doubts and fears were gone.

A nurse came over to my bed, I assumed to do additional pre-OP prep.

She sort of whispered to me, "I know you're the Miracle Girl. Would you mind telling me your story?"

It happens in the grocery store all the time; I don't know why all of the sudden the OR would be off-limits. So I told my story. She seemed satisfied.

They gave me the drugs, rolled me into the surgery, and I hosted my own liquidation sale in which everything had to go: adhesions, scarring, polyps, cysts, fibroids, endometriosis, bleeding and clotting abnormalities...all gone.

It was a much more involved surgery than the standard hysterectomy, which meant that my recovery was longer and slower, too. During those weeks and months, another layer was peeled. I started to see myself as a whole person, a complete woman, no longer a patient in limbo between surgeries, or a test case with compartmentalized parts of some society-driven model.

Finally, I was the best version of me. I was also super psyched not to have whiskers or extreme sweating. All those things I told myself about settling or not being enough—the opposite of what I tell everyone else I meet—no longer served a purpose in my head, which freed up my mind to get back to work as a professional, a title I felt I hadn't measured up to either.

I asked my mom how she really felt about not being a grandmother, me not birthing a baby and potentially not ever having a child; my path in life seemed to embody the act of mothering, not necessarily becoming a mother in the traditional sense. She didn't even pause.

She patted my rescue dog on the head and gently said, "I have Dolly."

In that moment, I felt I was a true feminist—a humanist, even—one who would never let anyone overpower me or my convictions. I got all hopped up on my own enlightenment and made the mistake of going online to view a video of a hysterectomy. (Don't do that). Blood and guts never bothered me before.

What I hadn't factored in was the out-of-body experience, the emotional fallout from the acknowledgement that this very intimate part of my body had been injured and treated like a science project repeatedly over the years, rarely in conjunction with love or out of my own desire. In a flash, a very non-medical event filled my brain.

I had been in a friend's wedding and a bunch of us went out afterward to continue partying. I met up with a guy I knew from the neighborhood, and we got talking and decided to go to another bar. Once there, I quickly determined it was not my scene and asked to go home.

The next thing I knew, I was in a cab going in the opposite direction of my apartment. I was very foggy and couldn't find my credit cards or purse. I tried to tell him I wanted to be dropped off at home. He didn't listen. It was the middle of the night when we pulled up to an apartment I'd never seen in a neighborhood I didn't know. I had no money, no phone, and I was in a bridesmaid dress. I had the presence of mind to decide that I might be better off inside than out on the street, so I willingly entered the front door.

I was trying to absorb things like the layout of the place, windows, anything. Everything was blurry. Every fiber of my being knew I was not safe. He offered the bed to me so I could rest. I didn't want to lie down, yet I was somehow powerless and felt my head sort of melt into the pillow. I pulled myself into a ball, tucked my head into my knees.

I don't know how long I was there but I woke up to him on top of me, one hand holding my face into the bed, the other trying to pry my knees apart. The upper part of my body was pinned down so I couldn't push up. I crossed my ankles. He started swearing and hitting me. Somehow, in a seemingly swift motion, he was midair at the same time I was able to wrench my body around, swinging my right arm up and out, delivering a blow that knocked him off the bed. I swirled towards the front door but couldn't maneuver the locks.

I felt his hands on me. I relinquished slightly. He dragged me over the couch, threw me into the wall next to it, all the while spewing vulgar demands. Then he went to the bathroom and passed out.

Minutes later, I was in a diner using a pay phone to call a friend. I was able to get on a bus with the promise that payment would be at the other end. I got home, showered and met the rest of the wedding party for breakfast. My arm was throbbing. A couple of my buddies offered to go find this guy and kill him, which in its own way was very sweet.

I only told a couple people about that night. I wasn't sure I had the right to feel traumatized since I hadn't been raped. I mean, I actually fought the guy off, so didn't that make it more of an altercation than an assault? The answer is no.

By comparison, maybe my hysterectomy and sexual assault don't appear to be connected; one event seems to have been a choice and one was not. In one, I was a victim and in the other, wasn't I also a victim? I share because I think we are too comfortable allowing certain aspects of both sides of our stories to needlessly devalue us. We are both, we are all, we are everything. If you let someone else dictate, you could lose out on a role you were born to play.

Chosen

Think of this as a tear-out card, like for a recipe or an exercise move, that you tuck in your wallet for the days you want to start fresh. When you're ready to see the ways in which you've been chosen, what that can look like for you in your world, keep these tips handy.

Here we go.

Be ready to be everything and nothing all the time:

Face every day knowing that you may have to respect authority, question authority and be the authority. In that same vein, you will need to follow rules, ignore rules and write rules, too. Being chosen means taking in what's around you, assessing the needs and knowing how best to solve problems. It's rarely as simple as condemning or condoning; but there's pretty much always a chance to show compassion.

Do it for the one:

If you need a crowd or a megaphone, you might need to rethink your mission statement. Whether I am speaking to an auditorium of people or a woman in the checkout line at the store, my value for our time and space is the same. Take your job seriously, not yourself. Speak your truth—the ones who need to hear you will.

Beware the invisible fence:

For every person to whom you give love freely, brace yourself for the ones who assault everything from your outfit to your belief system. Faith is essentially the acceptance of the unknown. As we move through the world though, there are things we can't unsee. These things require a thicker human skin, a kind of faith, too.

Repeatedly preaching to people who aren't ready to hear you is not the best use of your time. You may convince yourself you're a missionary, but in effect, it's more like being a dog in a zap collar running repeatedly into the electric fence. The outcome you might wish to achieve is change; however, doing the same thing over and over again expecting a different result is not faith, it's insanity. Perseverance—more closely resembling faith—requires you to find a unique and new tact when facing obstacles.

Practice equal parts ignorance and arrogance:

This does not mean hiding, bulldozing or grandstanding; you should be neither a troglodyte nor an erudite. Rather, hone the craft of learning when to speak and when to listen. There will be some conversations in which you actually say nothing at all. Your voice is sacred; so is your silence.

Keep your fat pants and your skinny jeans:

Each time you have an awakening, one that leaves you feeling forever changed, trust that parts of you will always remain. None of it should be ignored. The process is imperative to the product. All of it makes you, you.

Encore

"Mom always said, 'Use your words.'
I've had the great fortune to share my story
with people who took care of me
and people who will take care of others.
Here are some excerpts from speeches I've given
and a sneak peek at my next project.
Enjoy."

We Are Bl

I was given a timeframe of 12 minutes for my address. I spent weeks crafting what I would say. I've always been able to put words together with less time and a little extra fire under me, but for this, the opportunity was layered. I needed to say something to them as much as I needed to do it for me.

A former patient's daughter—who is a friend—offered to film the speech, in case I wanted to use it later for talks. (In the midst of all my doubts and therapeutic self-talk, I was certain that I would be speaking and creating a business from it.) All the technical equipment was in place and I'd been given my instructions about plugging and unplugging the microphone.

I stood at the microphone, my arms and legs numb. My vision and hearing were technically functioning, but I couldn't see or hear anything. I'd rehearsed and knew I was a little over time, but my experience taught me the adrenaline would likely make up for it. Each typed line had pen notes in the margin, reminding me to breathe.

I looked up, scanned, smiled, changed my cadence based on topic, remembered my inflections and did everything an engaging speaker should do. Rarely did I actually address the whole auditorium, because the seniors and I made a pact that it would be just us. There's always a way to create intimacy and unity.

When I finished my remarks, I looked for the cords to plug and unplug, and returned to my seat.

I'd taken 18 minutes, and internalized it as a catastrophe. In an instant, I devalued my message on a technicality, completely negating in my own life what I'd impressed upon the audience.

It wasn't until the next week that I could even look at the video. I'd gotten a standing ovation, and hadn't even seen it.

Here's some of what I shared.

While I didn't articulate it as such, I wanted to earn a lead role in this community, not have it handed to me. And that's

what the miracle was to me at 14, a title that served no purpose in the context of recovering from illness that had stripped me of all my controls and any semblance of normalcy.

What I didn't know then was the true value of an ensemble cast. A group of strangers befriended me, cared about me, prayed for me, laughed with me and wiped my tears. Brainiacs, Jocks, Clowns, Ingénues, Sidekicks, Villains, Lovers, Loners. I often pushed them all away.

It's hard not to feel like it's about me. In the journey from table read to closing night, egos can create unnecessary conflict and competition, which can result in a confidence breakdown for the actors. But when the ensemble works together, everything gels; and regardless of egos, the audience sees a final product of something that appears effortless, powerful, beautiful, inspiring and entertaining.

There can be no story without community, and there can be no community without story.

Members of the class of 2014, look around at your fellow graduates—is there someone who you can't bear to say goodbye to? Someone you want to say, good riddance? Someone who deserves an apology, a thank you or forgiveness? Perhaps that someone is you? Maybe not. Perhaps it's the person next to you.

We had senior superlatives, too. So know that in this batch of best dressed, nicest smile and most likely to be seen on a Friday night, there's also a loneliest, least recognized, most compassionate, strongest spirit.

How does it feel to be wearing this cap and gown? Who helped you get here? Who didn't? Remember, if Why then also Why Not? Coach not only let me suit up for varsity soccer, but my name was on the roster—with two leg braces, chronic asthma and nerve damage, I spent all but two minutes on the bench over the course of my four years here. My teammates called me Mama Mahoney. And I'm proud to say, this Mama lettered in varsity soccer as a senior. In your perception, did I earn it? Maybe. Maybe not.

Who are you without the label of athlete, artist, graduate? Who are you in your heart, where no one else but you lives? Whatever your answer, it matters... It matters.

Having gotten to know you a little bit over the last few weeks, you are insightful and thoughtful individuals. In many ways, you have already made your mark on the world. Your stories are unfinished, though you may feel defined in the eyes of many for what you have or have not achieved. I'm familiar with that. My life continues to be a series of decisions made in a delicate balance, influenced by my faith and experiences.

You, ladies and gentlemen, are more than ready for whatever lies ahead. In this moment in time, right now, you are the class of 2014. Time is an opportunity for togetherness. Nothing more. Nothing less. Never will this group of people share in the same time and space again in history. Think about that.

You will hold reunions, but not all of you will attend.

The destination is the big miracle, but without awareness on the journey, you miss out on all the little miracles along the way.

Pay attention.

You are a generation, and when I say that I now feel that I have lived in biblical times... you have instant resources in technology. Do you really know who provides the context or the history? Do you actually get to control your memories simply because something is theoretically erased with the click of a button? Does having GPS mean that you aren't allowed to get lost? Where's the adventure in that? What's the point if there's no joy along the way? Besides, how can you even appreciate success if you don't experience failure?

To clarify, the dream isn't failure, you're welcome.

Don't let fear of mistakes prevent you from making a choice. We're all afraid. The choices are only mistakes if you don't learn from them or keep repeating them. Will I play the rear-end of a life-size rhinoceros in 80-degree heat, again? I will not. But what a gift that I know that. A miracle really. See what I did there? Change the narrative.

In the world of a 24-hour media cycle, the concentric circles of news, gossip and opinion effectively blur the lines between reality and entertainment. It's a challenge to hear, heed and trust your own voice. None of us can truly be absent from the circumstance of humanity. None of us can run away from our own truth, even if it's a miracle. We end up where we are supposed to be.

When I graduated, I knew where I was heading: to college—a place that didn't require math—because let's be honest, that skill set was not part of my miracle.

I walked out of this gym thrilled to put it all behind me. I vowed I'd never come back.

I focused on what I didn't have. I needed more time on my journey to return today with true gratitude and honesty and joy.

When you leave today, you have a choice to take the values of your faith beyond these walls, or leave them behind.

Community—wherever you create it—is a gift. Engaging in it means being accountable, being culpable. It isn't easy. It isn't safe. And it isn't possible without risk.

This choice is one of many you will make in your adult lives. Whether you have grown in your Catholic faith or are struggling in it, you represent something greater than yourselves right now. That's what an ensemble cast is. That's what faith is.

Diplomas aside, faith isn't about understanding; it's about acceptance. It isn't about condemning or condoning; it's about compassion. Judgment has no place in growth.

What does help us grow? Dialogue, different opinions, thoughtful discussion. Again, risk.

Whatever your path, ladies and gentlemen, know that I can't wait to see how many ways you change our world. Because you're going to. You already have.

And, if you need guidance, ask Saint Marianne Cope. I have a hunch she'll see you through.

Thank you and congratulations.

Every Day Is Nurse's Day

I've had the great honor and pleasure of attending and speaking to students in colleges of nursing. I geek out with excitement every time. Here's a version of my remarks from one such ceremony.

It is 1985-ish. My class takes a trip down the hall to Mrs. Noone's room. She is the librarian. We are there to pick out a biography, which we will read, discuss and ultimately present.

I was captivated by the story of one woman's place in history, her model of caring for all in a time of war, her passion, commitment and perseverance in the face of so much unknown.

Florence Nightingale nestled into the depths of my heart and made a home in the recesses of my mind back then. I didn't realize the soul connection until much later.

It is 1992: meet my gynecological oncology nurses.

Debbie read me excerpts from my book.

Laura painted my nails and had spa days for me during chemo.

Annie threw marshmallows at me during my first blood transfusion.

Gerry, gruff but gentle and secure, taught me how to play gin rummy.

Allison, she was dating a resident. We liked him.

Lindy was a supervisor, caregiver and comic relief extraordinaire.

Noreen, like a humming bird, visited me at the beginning and end of her shift, whether I was in her care or not.

Today, Mother Marianne Cope is in the Hall of Fame for her knowledge and application of universal precautions, but in life and then death, she basically had privileges at all the hospitals. She was a devout force to be reckoned with.

It wasn't until I trained as a home health aide that I bonded with my deceased friend, a woman I'd never met, who would later become a saint known to all as the saint who saved my life. I think I was flagged as the Miracle Girl.

I raised my hand each time the teacher asked, "Has anyone ever known someone who has had..."

Pick a category.

I lived through multi-system organ failure. I was more prepared than I realized to go out in the field. Armed with my acting background, I auditioned in doorways and front hallways of stranger's homes, convincing them I could shake their hand, make them a meal and get them in the shower—all in under an hour, no rush.

I wasn't long for that track as a professional; my parents' respective illnesses required me to be the round-the-clock caregiver.

I'm grateful for the training.

But let's go back again. I had this fancy, not-yet-official miracle. What did that mean to me at 14, coming out of a coma and into a new town, new school and basically new body that couldn't do what it used to before I got sick?

It is March 1993: my nurse brothers and sisters and my nurse mothers and fathers are there. Ginger wheels me out to the elevator. Amy brings balloons. Barb, Adele, Doris, Linda, Kim, Terry...they line the halls and send me off.

Every cell in my body was excited, ready to leave. I hadn't factored in that eight months in the hospital meant no one else really knew what I'd been through. The nurses were my wisdom and secret keepers. They were my trainers, cheerleaders, validation; they were my reality. In the hospital, I was me, Kate. Outside the hospital I was The MIRACLE GIRL.

I was still in a wheelchair, wearing leg braces to counteract my atrophy-induced foot drop, unable to hold a pencil or a cup, due to chemo-related neuropathy. My voice was weak and quiet because of the intubation scarring.

From my book report to those early days of my recovery—and every day since—I have found my solace, my inspiration and my respect for all people through the eyes and the world of nursing.

I'm not a nurse. I still can't do math, and unfortunately it's not from the cardiac arrest or subsequent oxygen deprivation. A voracious reader, my fifth grade math report card said, "D+ but a pleasure to have in class."

Think about what it means to be right here, right now. You are making your history.

When you graduated, you transitioned from top of the heap to new kid again in your respective places of employment. Where did you go? Who have you met? What has happened there?

After all, you have learned there is still much that remains unknown.

You are Florence.

Under that same umbrella of why I love nurses: I have witnessed legacy within the walls of many care facilities... not simply welcoming all, but mandating that dignity, compassion, respect be part of the care.

You are Mother Marianne.

You are going to end up where you are supposed to be, whether you can see it fully or not. The notion of perfection is more than a little unsettling, especially in a field affected more often than others by life and death. Trust yourselves. Have faith.

Take the job seriously, and not yourself. I have some experience with this.

You've taken your tests; you know your charts, symptoms and program passwords. Please, embrace the concept of lifetime learning: all the highs and lows, roadblocks, mistakes, celebrations and milestones. You care for people and work with people from all walks of life. From beginning to end, there are moments worthy of building upon, moving past, healing through and reveling in.

Now, maybe you're squeezing ketchup onto the hotdog of a patient who's sipping his soda, completely baffled by his hypertension diagnosis, or cleaning soiled chuck pads from the bowel prep lady.

You may not always access gratitude or empathy, but you know you need humor, right? Depending on the day, it's a sliding scale of silliness to sardonic wit to general amusement of reality.

In a given shift, you are required to assess, act, engage and support. I don't know why a special soundproof room hasn't been mandated on floors of all medical institutions for the staff. Really, imagine the stress relief if you knew that for a minute a day, you could throw yourself into a wall, scream and throw things, and then fix your hair and go back on the floor?

It is February 1993, early in the morning, before the shift change. Laurie sits at my bed, while I recover from multiple seizures.

She reads to me. She does not leave my side.

Ladies and gentlemen, my hope for you—wherever you go—is that you find balance in your work life and your home life. For every patient to whom you give your all, there's a part of you that deserves the same respect and energy. You know why you chose this profession and you know what motivates you and scares you. I ask that you feel it all, honor it all, utilize it all. What got you here today is what makes you, you. Having been on the receiving end of countless incredibly caring, talented nurses, I'm honored always to be in your presence.

You are a part of my story. You are a part of my miracle.

That matters. You matter.

Thank you.

Til' Then

Thank you for your time and focus on this window into my world. I hope that I have left you with something to contemplate, added a little humor to your life, and imparted a sense that we are all miracles, even if that's still not what you'd call it. This book's intention is to encourage everyone to understand that their voice matters, and to serve as the impetus for conversation. There is always more to say.

A Caregiver's Voice

Below is a little something I'm playing with for my next book, tentatively titled, *It's Crisis, but with Jazz Hands.*

My parents' initial diagnoses with cancer were within 10 days of one another. All I knew about liver cancer was that people die and die quickly… like in weeks.

My mom's margins were clean, and her staging manageable with radiation and medications. She chose treatment in Syracuse for breast cancer. My father's cancer required more invasive procedures and specialists; therefore, he was directed to New York City. I received such thorough training as a patient-in-crisis years earlier. I possessed the faith to ask why and why not in the same breath. Still, the cancer "tsunami" most certainly swallowed me up as well.

For about a month, I drove back and forth from Syracuse to NYC a few times each week. I was able to wake in the wee hours of the morning to work out, tidy up, prepare meals in the blender for the dog and dress the cat. Yes, in keeping with our theme of sublime to ridiculous, our 19-year-old dog was mostly toothless, and our kitten with eczema required clothing. You know when you see a building that's been condemned and officials have blocked the unsafe area with caution tape? We lived in such constant crisis; it was as if our home was wrapped in metaphorical caution tape.

My mom made it to remission having survived the burns, the scars and the manhandling that followed her through her breast cancer. She endured a brain tumor diagnosis, surgery and recovery weeks after we buried my father. She guided me gracefully, putting one foot in front of the other. My father lived nine and half years with primary liver cancer that carried with it terrifying, humiliating symptoms and side effects, including a few strokes. The doctors told us that while there was nothing more they could do, he had blown the statistics out of the water.

I intended to contact everyone personally about status changes. After all, I was raised knowing that you're as good as your word. And you should use your words; people like the sound of their own name, and 95 percent of life is showing up.

I attempted to hold down jobs and attend rehearsals and auditions during all of this. As his care required more of a hands-on approach, I had to shift gears. I began email updates to friends and family. The list grew as my messages were forwarded to the concentric circles of people he had collected over the years. As his status declined, so did mine: asthma, anxiety, depression, obesity, high blood pressure. I walked around for days on end looking like a "before picture."

As the replies came in, reaching out to share my role as caregiver through these emails became my refuge, my therapy and my reward. It was part of my new and full-time job.

My cousin once said to me, "I don't want this to sound bad, but I can't wait to get home after work to read what you've sent us!"

After my father's death, I was out shopping and a woman stopped me and said, "You don't know me, but I've been on your email list. We send them around the office!"

At his eulogy, a young Congressman my dad had mentored declared that we needed to change how we approach death from cancer because my father didn't lose a battle with the disease; he won. And he taught us all more about living in the process.

My father, for all his lobbying, campaigning and advance-man capabilities, was first and foremost a mentor, so the fact that this young man gleaned from him such a powerful and sustaining life lesson to me is just one more reason he was on earth as long as he was. My mother and I have talked about it. We miss this man of our house every day and wish he was walking around with us, sharing in our experiences in a more tangible way.

Something deep inside knows that he wasn't meant to be with us on earth a minute more or less.

In the weeks before my father's death and before my mom's brain tumor diagnosis, we had solidified a new normal, which mandated brutal honesty, equal amounts of tears and laughter, and a silent resignation to a routine that often took me to the store without a bra, clean hair or brushed teeth.

In the following pages, you will see part of my journey: emails sent out to update our friends and family that bear the truth of the caregiver roles, and just what happened during this timeframe.

Update: John Mahoney
Morning all.

First, you need to know that Pop is still here, still kickin' and we are all faring well.

Other than a teaspoon, in four servings, of hot cereal—which he requested—Pop's had no food. He has been taking in fluids, very sparingly, but that's keeping him comfortable. He is a little more verbal than last week and has been participating in phone calls and visits as his energy allows him.

I assure you, just because he's dying doesn't mean he's not annoying. And just because he is sad to leave us doesn't mean he's not sick of our faces.

At any given time, the phone rings, the emails come in, and a friend walks through the door. These people wishing to reach out to him, to us, outside of our relationship, don't always have anything in common. Yet hasn't that always been Pop's legacy? Connecting people.

I've lived in Syracuse longer than I've lived anywhere else; but because illness has always been a key factor in decision making, I've never felt like I could put roots down here. Odd, given that so much of my family is here.

The 'ban' on quiet, scheduling and rules is lifted, and we three Mahoney's have done more living with living than living with dying, despite the total sleep deprivation and chapped lips due to the dehydration that accompanies crying, carbs and sweets.

I don't feel like a visitor anymore. And I know that will only serve me in the future.

I took the overnight shift Tuesday and pulled Pop's hospital bed over to my bed, shoving pillows in between the frames to make one big bed. He put his arms around me and I said, "I'm so glad we've said everything we need to say." We lay there in silence, listening to the pounding rain on the roof.

I listened to him breathing and let my head rise and fall on his chest. And there they were again, more things to say. I meandered through memories of the two of us sitting on the glider on my grandparent's porch up in Henderson Harbor during storms. Mom and Gramma would warn us not to go out in the wind and the rain, but we would bundle up and snuggle, while getting only slightly wet and cold.

Then I realized that we were in this familiar place, imminent death aside. Our breath was the same.

When I was little and he would read to me from a collection of linguistic wonders, I always found myself trying to breathe the same way he was as I lay on his chest. And I always felt a sense of accomplishment when I could train my little lungs to meet his.

I was spewing all these thoughts as I was thinking them and finally I said to him, "Are you tired?"

With all the strength he had he said, "YES."

I said, "Do you want me to shut up?"

Again, "YES."

"Do you love me?"

"Yes."

I was only a couple hours and we were awake again, but it was one of the best night's sleep I've ever had.

Wednesday morning my mom had the breakdown: the ugly cry, the heaving and snotting and the words that can only come when a person is pushed to the limit. She crawled in bed with Pop and I closed the door.

How relieved I was to know that my parents had that moment.

It's kind of like when you're a kid and you see your parents kiss for the first time and don't know what it means but know how it makes you feel.

It's all tingly happiness, and for me, a feeling of great safety and security amidst a lot of unknowns.

The model of my parents' marriage has set me up as much for success as it has failure. They've inspired me to a degree I'm not always sure I'll measure up or achieve, let alone sustain—this kind of respect, humor, admiration, patience and adventure in a relationship.

"In your travels, do you think you can find me a husband?" I choked up and squeezed Pop's hand, adding "No one will ever take care of me the way you have taken care of me...but this experience has taught me that I know what I need and I know what I want; more than that, you've taught me how to ask for it...so, if you see someone who might give me these things, give 'em a nudge. OK?"

He rubbed my hand, smiled, then got serious and firmly said, "Deal."

That's it.

Love, Kate

Update: Mary Mahoney

There's no easy way to say this and I'm sorry to send it in an email. I guess I'm picking up where I left off.

My mom has a brain tumor. Technically, it's a tumor in the brain and it is believed to be benign.

I feel a little like that obscure company whose catalogue you ordered mittens from nine years ago, and subsequently get other catalogues and emails enticing you with everything from deals on loom supplies to seasonally festive toilet paper caddies to desk lamps that are somehow also GPS trackers and beverage dispensers. You don't need any of these things, but you read through because you're curious.

As many of you know, Mom had cataract surgery in June, just hours before Pop's first massive stroke. And you know that she's been getting tests done and talking to the doctors for a couple of months.

We are very lucky she had the cataract surgery, and such diligent and caring doctors. When the eye guy couldn't identify the problem a month or so ago, he set Mom up with a neurologist who ordered an MRI and scans to see, no pun intended, if there was anything going on behind the eye.

It's brain surgery, literally, so her head will have to be partially shaved and her skull will be drilled in to. If the tumor is resting on the optic nerves, it will essentially be 'lifted' and removed. If it is attaching to the nerve, the goal is still removal, but it will be more time consuming and a little more involved. Risks are everything from standard post-surgical reactions to death. No emotions, just facts.

We don't know what the future holds, so we are working with what's right in front of us and little more.

To make a long story longer, I found out about this tumor in the doctor's office after looking at a scan and asking, "What is that gray area?" and he said, "That's the tumor." I looked to Mom for a response and she was not shocked. She has known for a month or so and wanted to protect me while we buried and grieved Pop.

Mom has a camel-like capacity for emotion and information, of which I am in constant awe.

Mom told the doctor that I was just learning all this. He looked at her and said, "Did she say she just wanted you to tell the truth?... Is that because you taught her that when she was 5? ...These things...They come back to you..."

We both left feeling very comfortable with the doctor. I genuinely felt like he would do everything with his skill set, and would do it well, for my mother. For me, beyond that I can't ask for more from a surgeon. The prayer is what helps the final outcome, and we learned that with Pop.

Our brand of 'normalcy' resumed.

Here's an excerpt of our conversation on the way home.

[In the car, we look at each other and simultaneously exclaim] "Thank God He's Dead!"

Mom: "What if I wake up and I'm blind or my legs don't work?"

Me: "I will smother you with a pillow."

Mom: "Oh, good... Will you be sad if I die?"

Me: "Are all the papers in my name?"

Mom: "Yes."

Me: "So they won't do an autopsy. Wait. Have I just smothered you with the pillow or did you just die anyway?"

Mom: "I just died anyway."

Me: "I will be very sad, but I won't be looking at jail time, so I'll be okay. Seriously, I can't control whether or not you die. I can only work with right now... Of course, I could have worked with right now a month or so ago, before you chose to lie to me repeatedly..."

Mom: (very content sigh) "Go left and stop at the store on the way home. I want chicken for dinner."

My friends, you can label it shock or coping mechanisms, but I will be very surprised if Mom and I are able to make any new friends when this is all over, and I will likely be speaking in clicks and tones.

We know you're there and that you are likely as blown away by all of this as we are. Please give us the space to get to things in our own time.

I will be in touch very soon.

Love,

Kate and Mary

Update: Mary Mahoney

Hi all,

Mom has had a great week! The nurse has been in twice to assess her incision, and it is healing at the right pace: slow. We tackled the shower, which was a combination of boundaries completely destroyed as the shower chair seemed to slide down the floor of the tub, as though a current were pulling it.

After a lot of laughing, crying and yelling, we realized it was the result of some bath oil.

It's amazing that this very major brain surgery was the equivalent to going to the drive-thru, but her body and mind are still in recovery mode. To say nothing of the recovery she/we are just beginning to experience in life without my dad.

A few days ago, I found myself sitting in the living room staring at the wall. I think I sat there for almost an hour. It was oddly rejuvenating to realize that wall didn't need me. It was surprising that I could spend almost an hour staring at a wall and I was perfectly comfortable knowing that was all I could handle. Mom did the same thing in her bedroom.

I think I've said this to you all before, but it's different now. We are wrapping our heads around this new normal. And I think, despite the void, we are ready for it.

I, with my stress-induced high blood pressure, obesity, asthma and arthritis, got on the treadmill today. I turned on my playlist of songs that were seemingly popular when I last listened to it on the treadmill about four years ago in Chicago.

I sweat out everything from red velvet cake to feelings, and as the endorphins kicked in I remembered what discipline for myself used to be about. I picked up my pace and practiced my awards show power walk. I truly felt healthy for the first time in years, whole years. After about 45 minutes though, my forward-thinking attitude changed, and I felt a great kinship with the wounded or hunted Big Game in the wilderness.

But enough of my journaling. Mom is well. She tires easily and is anxious to see the doctor next week to get his perspective.

I'll check in after that appointment and we'll go from there.

Love and prayers,
Kate

I'd Like To Thank My Academy

I dreamed of hearing my name called, gracefully and swiftly, and making my way to the stage to accept my award, wearing a red satin gown. However, part of that dream was about using my platform as an award winner to be an agent of change and good in my community, and in the world. My performance trajectory in Chicago was halted when I moved back home and in with my parents to become their aide. I practiced my red-carpet saunter on the treadmill in the wee hours of the morning, before the caregiving began. One morning, a spider dropped from the ceiling, within inches of my face. I lost my balance and the treadmill threw me into the wall. I landed in a heap. I stayed in some semblance of said heap for a long time.

I know I did a lot alone to get myself back up, but the fact remains, I would not have this life or the opportunities that will come from it without a community of artists, friends, family, coworkers and faithful support.

This is my thank you to my academy.

Mom, you are the best roommate I've ever had. I may have to have you cloned or frozen. At the very least, I'll make sure your admitting packet includes all your favorites.

To the Mahoney granddaughters, you've taught me a lot about sisterhood, motherhood and womanhood. I'm proud to be the lil'st one. Thank you for the blackout memories. Cheers to the Gigger!

To RT and Marion's clan, I still don't know how to play pitch. Thank you for not kicking me out of the family. I love how we love each other.

Juge, Pete, Gemma (my bff), Bookie, Charlie and James Francis, you helped me get this show on the road. Seriously, thank you.

To Rose and Tom's tribe, I can't wait to have breakfast with you, so we can talk about what to have for lunch. Thank you for living all over the country so no matter where I am, I can feel like I'm home.

To my Alexandria and Rosemont family, you were my first teachers, first friends, first teammates. A part of my heart will always be on Russell Road.

To all my ACDS family, you were the first people with whom I performed. I definitely wouldn't have made it this far without you.

To my SAS gals, I still can't believe I was only in school with you for one year. Thank you for continuing to nourish our friendships. If I get called up, I'll rely on one of our many dance routines for my audition. Abby, remember that time we went to Italy? #giftoftears

To all the lads in Limerick, when I am with ye, sure it's like no time has passed at all. You were part of my most grand adventures. Slainte!

To my hospital and therapy family from 1992, 1993 and all the recovery years, words don't do justice to my gratitude. Of course, there was a miracle, I had all of you. Thank you.

To my BL family, after such incredible trauma, I needed a good 15 years of distance to gain perspective. I couldn't say it then, but thanks for the prayers, and the Varsity letter even though I sat on the bench.

To my fellow Shoremen, thank you for coming to my party. Seriously though, I'd be lost without you. And to all who frequented the Bird, the birthplace of the first draft of my show, thanks for the bottles and bowls of booze.

To my Chicago family, like the Clark bus with all its characters and misadventures, I need you to get where I am going. Love and gratitude.

To all my holistic, allopathic and empathetic practitioners who saw me through several lifetimes of trials, thank you.

To all my friends and neighbors in the Syracuse community, our ancestors paved the way for us to have a better life. Thank you for doing the same for all those we welcome in the years to come. Thank you for your support and kindness.

To my improv, theatre and film family, the job of writing a show—building a set, lighting the way, telling the story, managing creative people—is a noble one. Thank you for allowing me to share in that with you from time to time. Continued leg breaking to you all!

To all the people who hired me and employed me over the years, thanks for taking a chance on me. Be it WC, Spanners, MGR, Hillbrook, the Great NY State Fair, the Grande Cuisine, VG, Lettuce, AVI, countless babysitting, house sitting and pet sitting resume builders, I think we can all agree I was meant to welcome people and tell stories. I'll leave it at that.

Hail, Girls

Sisters, where do I begin?

For me, the thought of becoming a nun seemed like a thought that was supposed to be. Why? Because of the miracle?

I struggled with feelings of confusion and not belonging or leading or following. I thought maybe because people told me I was chosen to receive this miracle of my recovery that it meant I should change my path, or solidify it, though I was still very young.

Today, when I look at my life overall—and I'm still young—I realize that my calling is to stay as I am, with my gratitude and devotion to Mother Marianne, my dedication to all patient and caregiver advocacy, and my deep and continued faith.

There is no question that we are in a challenging time in our Church. I can only say that I am continually inspired by you in your capacity to stay true to your own calling.

We are no longer a generation or community that speaks when spoken to or acts simply because we are told.

Leading by example and participating in dialogue are critical, and not just dialogue with like-minded people. Sharing different experiences, backgrounds and beliefs does not require or result in going against your beliefs. I have seen this modeled by so many of you.

In most instances, you stay very true to yourself. Your openness gives others a sense that we all have a lifetime of opportunities in which we can help, heal and guide all in the name of God.

Thank you for being present emotionally, spiritually and socio-politically.

Thank you for living the beatitudes.

Along those lines, thank you for teaching me how to rescue animals. You are good Franciscans!

Thank you for your energy and focus.

Remember that time in Rome when a few of us drank a little too much limoncello and almost missed the bus? You know who you are.

Remember when I called each of you sister to the point that it was embarrassing because I didn't know your real names after all those years? Thank you for letting me break the rule on that one. Thank you for letting me in your world, while you have celebrated mine.

The slumber party during Holy Week, before you moved from the Mother House to the Villa will go down as one of my most sacred—and fun—memories.

I hope you know how deeply I respect and admire each of you... all of you.

I grieve the sisters who have gone before us as well. Though like you, I trust they are at home with God, at peace.

Thank you for teaching me about gumption and grit.

I love you.

Fan Mail

We don't have matching jackets, monthly meetings or an official newsletter. Those of us bonded together by our individual miracles—our relationships with Mother Marianne—simply show up for one another. I don't do it in a traditional way. Life is busy. We can't always drop everything to be physically present, yet there is an unspoken understanding that we support one another from wherever we are, whenever we can. This is our faith in action.

So, dear teammates, you know who you are.

We have watched movies, painted each other's nails, tasted recipes, trained as co-workers.

We have connected via email and phone calls, even though we've never met.

I have visited you in hospitals, gone out to lunch with you, listened to you tell your story in the back of church halls.

We have talked at length about death, dying, loss and grief. Somehow we always end up laughing.

We are as devout as we are defiant, thank God.

I have buried you; it's a moment most of us experience, but will likely never get easier for me, when your loved ones ask me why juxtaposed with my existence.

Mother has been a divine puppet master, giving us everything from parking spots to a chance at new perspective or continued health.

Thank you, my soul sisters and brothers in miracles. Thank you for making me see that my existence is an equal miracle to my recovery. You remind me every day that my voice matters, that I matter.

This thing we all have? It's a pretty sweet deal.

Reflections On Mother Marianne Cope

Sister Rose Ann Renna, OSF, RN, MSN

It seems incredible that, after 60 years in our religious community, I can say I have known Mother Marianne for half of that time.

Typical of the stress on humility among sisters, it was not well known that this amazing woman did so much in her life and was such a leader at a time women were not expected to be leaders.

Although not entering our community until she was 24 years old, Mother Marianne wasted no time in doing good, finding the needs that were present and moving to alleviate the suffering she saw.

In 1863, Mother became a prime mover in the building of St. Elizabeth Hospital in Utica, NY, to address the needs of the poor and sick. In 1869, Mother again led the way in the procurement of a saloon and dance hall on Prospect Hill in the city of Syracuse, NY. This establishment was converted into a 15-bed hospital that cared for all persons "regardless of race, religion, or the ability to pay." In fact, payment was most often given in a type of bartering with bags of flour, sacks of beans, chickens, and other supplies needed by the sisters to feed the patients.

Patients who could pay were known to give sums such as one quarter or dollar per month. So frequently, in Mother's own writing in the patient register was the word, "Charity" to denote no payment. It is noteworthy that these two hospitals were the first in Central New York, and among the first 50 hospitals in the country.

Mother led the way in welcoming all: the poor, the homeless, the alcoholic, even the unwed mother. She was Mother of Outcasts long before having this title attributed to her at her canonization. She welcomed all and frequently was seen ministering to them at their bedsides.

Soon after taking over as Superintendent (Administrator) of St. Joseph Hospital in 1870, Mother engaged the help of other influential persons in moving the Medical School from Geneva,

NY to Syracuse, NY. Now, the students not only had a school, but a hospital in which to practice.

While Mother was generous and welcoming in her treatment of the students, she made it known that if any patient did not want to be cared for by a medical student, the request of the patient would be honored. Her honoring of the dignity of the person, even one who paid nothing for care, was always utmost to Mother.

It is said that Mother had such a grasp of pharmaceutical concepts that she could easily have been a pharmacist. Along with this skill, her awareness of the menace of an unclean environment led her to be very strict in the practice of sanitation, insisting on hand washing at a time that it was not considered necessary. It is not surprising that Mother's principles of cleanliness contributed greatly to the care of lepers when she reached Hawaii. In addition, no sister has ever contracted this disease.

How do we make Mother Marianne real?

This lovely woman was truly full of compassion, doing whatever necessary to bring comfort to the needy. This compassion brought her to the next phase of her life in her service to the truly outcasts: the lepers of Hawaii.

For more information on Saint Marianne Cope, please visit www.saintmarianne.org.

Acknowledgements

Thomas Moore, Fr. Richard Rohr, Cara Rotondaro McDonough, Sean Kirst, Mary Ellen Clausen, Alyssa LaFaro, and Allison Heishman, thank you for your endorsements and your support.

Sister RA, how blessed I am to count you as a soul friend. Thank you for sharing your words on Mother.

Marcus, Chris and the Pegasus team, your patience has been a virtue. Thank you for welcoming me and believing in my story.

Laura, we did it! Thank you for teaching me everything you know about everything, and then repeating it 100 times depending on where we were in the fits and starts. Thank you for sticking with me and helping me take flight.

To Beverly, Susan and all the authors in the Divine Phoenix stable who shared experiential knowledge, wisdom, friendship and even some editing, thank you.

Lorna, you are like a great ballad from an 80's hair band. I am so grateful for the opportunity to work and write together. Thank you.

Sarah, quite literally none of this would have happened without you. Thank you, my sister friend. I can't wait to see all the ways the world will become better because of you.

Lydia, thank you for catering to my vanity and insanity in the design process!

Zac, thank you for the webstravaganza. #nailedit.

Thanks to Jillain Pastella Salamone and Jillian Kane for my cover shoot hair and makeup.

Manny and Linda, thank you for your counsel as I navigated branding, business and the writing of this, my first book.

To Sheila, thank you for your guidance, spirit and belief that I could be awesome.

In Memoriam

Mother Marianne, we've been friends a while now — I think we have a good thing going. Thanks for literally being the voice in my head that helps me keep my chin up. Also, thanks for the parking spots, every time!

Sister Mary Laurence Hanley, you were Mother's biggest fan, fearing my post-modernist ways would upset the balance all the while. You taught me the importance of determination, the perils of divisiveness. I couldn't have become who I am or told this story without you. Thank you, my friend.

Pop, I miss you every single minute of every single day. Yet in so many ways, you are with me more now than ever. Thank you for your guidance both in life and in death. This book is a love letter to you and the life you lived with me and Mom.

To all who watch over me, be they family, old friends or new, thank you for the time you spent in my world and the blessing for me to be a part of yours.

Reader Discussion Questions

It is through our differences that we find our unity.

In the spirit of sharing dialogue, here's a little something to get you going.

1. Do you believe in Miracles?
2. Have you ever felt you weren't heard?
3. What is faith?
4. Fill in this blank: I will never_____.
5. How do you allow yourself permission to feel all your feelings?
6. What is your deepest fear?
7. What does it mean to you to be chosen?
8. Imagine you've just done what you said you'd never do in number 4. Discuss.
9. Make a list of all the things that make you, *you*. Hang on to the list.

Always remember you matter and you have a voice.
Please invite me to connect with you or your group by visiting www.katedmahoney.com.
Again, thank you.

About The Cover

My first babysitting job was for my next door neighbors' son. I was 10. Eric was a toddler. The first few times I took care of him, either his mother or my mother was in the house just in case. Sometimes I was given more responsibility and a night shift. Usually we'd watch movies; and after Eric went to bed, I'd turn all the lights in the house on, to ensure safe passage from room to room.

We loved to play with blocks and build couch forts, covering the space between the cushions and the coffee table with blankets to create caves and nooks in which to explore or hide. Outside, there was always the option of bike riding, kicking the soccer ball, climbing the tree forts and naming clouds.

In many cultures, this is known as sky gazing. We didn't have such a graceful name for it. In the era of *thank goodness it's Friday* (TGIF) appointment television, we called it cloud television. Eric and I would lie on the lawn, looking up at the clouds. We created a world from the characters we identified that changed as the wind moved them through the sky.

When I lay in a hospital bed years later, I received an envelope containing a cassette. Eric narrated for me. It was a very special episode of our once-famed cloud television.

I'm a sucker for sunrises and sunsets. Every day, I try not to miss either one. For me, there is possibility in the rise and gratitude in the setting. It grounds me even if the day in between is nothing but chaos, worry or doubt. I knew at the onset of this project; clouds would serve as a backdrop to my story.

Now about the halo.

The halo is not meant to offend. Rather it's to be thought of as a prop. Some people *need* the halo to be there when they meet me. Others feel I don't deserve it, and therefore perhaps it's slightly off-kilter. I looked at a version of the halo with a thinner, more delicate band, but that was too angelic. The point of the thick band is to convey the weight this label of "Miracle Girl" has often laid on me; cocking the halo to one side is my nod to taking the experience —not myself —seriously.

About The Author

Kate D. Mahoney is a miracle and she wants you to know you are, too. Even if that's not what you'd call it.

She's named after the feisty, independent character in William Shakespeare's *Taming of the Shrew,* and was born in Washington, D.C., to educators and activists. Sporting purple feet pajamas as a munchkin in the *Wizard of Oz,* Kate didn't know her role of a lifetime would ultimately be that of just being herself.

Kate spent her formative years in Alexandria, Virginia, and then the Republic of Ireland. While on summer vacation in her parent's birthplace of Central New York, she was diagnosed with stage four germ cell ovarian cancer and later experienced multi system organ failure. She was 14.

International and nondenominational prayer requests were directed to a deceased nun by the name of Mother Marianne Cope. Kate's discharge papers state her recovery from the organ failure could not be explained medically. Her case led to the canonization of Mother Cope, and an adventure that was as sacred as it was side-splittingly funny to Vatican City.

Kate holds a B.A. in drama from Washington College in Chestertown, Maryland, as well as certificates from iO Chicago and Second City. She is an international speaker and activist who travels the globe to share honest and humorous anecdotes from her life as patient and caregiver.

If you feel that this story intertwines with your own journey, please consider spreading the message of the *The Misfit Miracle: Candid Reflections* with a wider audience. Bring Kate to your hometown, share www.katedmahoney.com on your social networks, Skype with Kate for book clubs and/or schedule Kate for a keynote talk.

It is through our differences that we find our unity.

Connect at www.katedmahoney.com.

CPSIA information can be obtained
at www.ICGtesting.com
Printed in the USA
FFOW05n1933200317

9 781941 859582